# Quotable
# War Or Peace

Compiled & Edited by

## Geoff Savage

Sound And Vision

# TABLE OF CONTENTS

THE POLITICIAN.

"A Politician should (as I have read)
Be furnished in the first place with a head".
WILLIAM HOGARTH [1697-1764]
Printed in *Hogarth Works 1*, Published originally
in 1775. Reprinted by Jones and Co. London in 1833

# PREFACE

It is said that comedy is tragedy only later. But there has never been anything at all comedic about any war, no matter how long ago. Bemusing but certainly not amusing. Humorous things can happen to people during war-time or engaged in a war but war itself is not a source of merriment.

War once created heroes. A casper milquetoast selling ties at a large department store all his life has little chance of being a hero. And yet, put this same person in a battlefield situation and he is given the opportunity to become a hero. For reasons explained by psychiatrists and others, a person in a certain situation will rise to the occasion, even go well beyond the sense of reason and perform acts of unexplainable or un-reasoning heroism.

Cartoonists are busy during wartime putting clever and amusing words into the mouths of people in harm's way, often belittling the enemy as dim-witted. Coming readily to mind is the classic WW1 sketch by English cartoonist Bruce Bairnsfather, depicting two soldiers in a fox hole. With shells exploding all around and one says to his complaining comrade, "Well, if you knows of a better 'ole, go to it!"

This collection of quotations about war and peace records just some of the spontaneous one liners or sentences of com-batants, or observers, or the well crafted lines written for a person in authority or of influence. But there are no knee-slappers here. Incidentally, why were there so many sensitive poems written by soldiers in WW1 and not WW2?

A friend of mine, an ex Washington lawyer, was assigned to an aircraft carrier in World War II. He told me that they lectured the men every day to assuage any hesitation about killing Japanese, who, they were repeatedly told, were not human. He and his colleagues knew only too well that what they were preaching was a lie.

We visited an interesting war museum in Germany, where there were rows upon rows of medieval suits of armour. What

3

surprised us was that these warriors were small. None of the suits could have accommodated a person over five feet or perhaps 5'3." Then there were the swords and lances, etc. Today's man would be hard put to even lift one, let alone wield it. War then was a one-on-one affair and very strenuous, too.

*The Hundred Year's War* lasted for 116 years during time which those who started the war died, leaving the fighting to a new generation who, in turn, also passed it along. Centuries later, winning *The Six Day War* of June, 1967 took just that many days but, to this day, no one has won the peace.

British history includes the statistics of the Battle of Culloden of 1746 and we all knew about Bonnie Prince Charlie. We visited Edinburgh Castle and viewed the names of the people who fell, the various artifacts and a tattered banner. The overwhelming, tangible sadness of that human tragedy, the worst slaughter in Scottish history, hung over the room.

"It is a curious fact," to quote the Oxford English Dictionary, "that no Germanic nation in early historic times had in living use any word properly meaning 'war,' though several words with that meaning survived in poetry, in proverbial phrases, and in compound personal names. The Romantic-speaking peoples were obliged to use the Latin *bellum* (war) on account of its formal coincidence with *bello* (beautiful)."

Perhaps our heritage is to be regularly involved in a war of some scale or another graduating from sticks and stones to today's popular phrase, weapons of mass destruction. Whoever devised that rallying call knew exactly what was necessary to produce the desired result!

"Don't be so gloomy. After all it's not that awful," wrote Orson Welles for Harry Lime in The Third Man. "In Italy for thirty years under the Borgias they had warfare, terror, murder and bloodshed but they produced Michelangelo, Leonardo da Vinci, and the Renaissance. In Switzerland they had brotherly love; they had five hundred years of democracy and peace and what did that produce? The cuckoo clock!"

Bruce Surtees

# Dedication

From a proud father to his Sons and their Families:

Carl,
Maria & Abby
and
Jonathan,
Itsuko & Taiki

# War

Choose your friends carefully. Your enemies will choose you.

Yassir Arafat, Palestinian Leader (b.1929)

"To answer these attacks and rid the world of evil, We will export death and violence to the four corners of the earth in defense of this great nation." Grandiose visions. Woodward comments, The president was casting his mission and that of the country in the grand vision of God's Master Plan.

As quoted in Bob Woodward's, *Bush at War,* (2003)
George W. Bush, American President (b1946)

Join the Army! Travel to exotic, distant lands. Meet exciting, unusual people, and kill them.

Graffiti in Bromley

We can, for example, be fairly confident that either there will be a world without war or there won't be a world — at least, a world inhabited by creatures other than bacteria and beetles, with some scattering of others.

Noam Chomsky, American Author (b.1928)

We live in the time where we have fictitious election results that elects a fictitious president. We live in a time where we have a man sending us to war for fictitious reasons. Whether it's the fiction of duct tape or fiction of orange alerts we are against this war, Mr. Bush... And any time you got the Pope and the Dixie Chicks against you, your time is up.

Speech at the 2003 Oscars
Michael Moore, American Filmmaker (b1954)

The war in Iraq is a rare opportunity to move toward an historic period of cooperation. Out of these troubled times ... a new world order can emerge.

George W Bush, American President (b1946)

All wars are popular for the first thirty days.

Arthur Schlesinger Jr, American Author (b.1917)

War and culture, those are the two poles of Europe, her heaven and hell, her glory and shame, and they cannot be separated from one another. When one comes to an end, the other will end also and one cannot end without the other. The fact that no war has broken out in Europe for fifty years is connected in some mysterious way with the fact that for fifty years no new Picasso has appeared either.

Paul in *The Brilliant Ally of His Own Gravediggers.*
Milan Kundera, Czechoslovakian Author (b.1929)

I don't see us winning the war. We have made enemies of one billion Muslims.

Gore Vidal, American Author (b.1925)

A politician's job they say is very high, for he has to choose who's got to go and die. *N.I.B*

Black Sabbath, British Rock Band

All war represents a failure of diplomacy.
> Speech to House of Commons after the 1991 Gulf War
> Tony Benn, British Politician (b.1925)

Our leaders had the audacity to say the Gulf War made America feel good again. How morally corrupt are we that we need a war to feel good about ourselves?
> Tim Robbins, American Actor (b.1958)

It doesn't require any particular bravery to stand on the floor of the Senate and urge our boys in Vietnam to fight harder, and if this war mushrooms into a major conflict and a hundred thousand young Americans are killed, it won't be U.S. Senators who die. It will be American soldiers who are too young to qualify for the Senate.
> George McGovern, American Politician (b.1922)

It's the old who get us into war; it's the young who end up in body bags.
> Russell Simmons, American Hip Hop Artist (b.1942)

War should be the politics of last resort. And when we go to war, we should have a purpose that our people understand and support.
> Colin Powell, American Secetary of State (b.1937)

We are really appalled by any country, whether a superpower or a small country, that goes outside the United Nations and attacks independent countries.
*Newsday.*
> Nelson Mandela, South African President (b.1918)

I dream of giving birth to a child who will ask, "Mother, what was war?"
> Eve Merriam, American Poet (b.1916)

9

They not only want to go into Iraq and disarm and overthrow this regime. They want to make Iraq a satellite of the U.S., democratize it and use it as a base camp for modernizing the Arab and Islamic world. That is imperialism pure and simple.

Pat Buchanan, American Journalist (b.1938)

Let someone else get killed! Suppose everyone on our side felt that way? Well then I'd certainly be a damned fool to feel any other way, wouldn't I? Englishmen are dying for England, Americans are dying for America, Germans are dying for Germany, Russians are dying for Russia. There are now fifty or sixty countries fighting in this war. Surely so many countries can all be worth dying for? Anything worth living for, said Nately, is worth dying for. And anything worth dying for, answered the old man, is certainly worth living for. *Catch 22*, (1961)

Joseph Heller, American Author (1922-1999)

If we lose this war, oil will be $100 a barrel, and if we win, it will be like $25 a barrel.

Donald Rumsfeld, American Defense Secretary (b.1935)

War is, after all, the universal perversion. We are all tainted: if we cannot experience our perversion at first hand we spend our time reading war stories, the pornography of war; or seeing war films, the blue films of war; or titillating our senses with the imagination of great deeds, the masturbation of war.
*The Custard Boys*, (1960)

John Rae, British Author (b.1931)

The greatest crime since World War II has been U.S. foreign policy.

Ramsey Clark, American Lawyer (b.1927)

10

Bitter after being snubbed for membership in the "Axis of Evil", Libya, China and Syria today announced that they had formed the "Axis of Just as Evil", which they said would be more evil than that stupid Iran-Iraq-North Korea axis President Bush warned of in his State of the Union address. Axis of Evil members, however, immediately dismissed the new Axis as having, for starters, a really dumb name. "Right. They are just as evil ...in their dreams!" declared North Korean leader Kim Jong-il. "Everybody knows we're the best evils ... best at being evil ... we're the best."Diplomats from Syria denied they were jealous over being excluded, although they conceded they did ask if they could join the Axis of Evil."They told us it was full," said Syrian President Bashar al-Assad. An axis can't have more than three countries", explained Iraqi President SaddamHussein. "This is not my rule, it's tradition. In World War II you had Germany, Italy, and Japan in the evil Axis. So, you can only have three, and a secret handshake. Ours is wickedly cool."International reaction to Bush's Axis of Evil declaration was swift, as within minutes, France surrendered. Elsewhere, peer-conscious nations rushed to gain triumvirate status in what has become a game of geopolitical chairs. Cuba, Sudan and Serbia announced that they had formed the "Axis of Somewhat Evil", forcing Somalia to join with Uganda and Myanmar in the "Axis of Occasionally Evil", while Bulgaria, Indonesia and Russia established the "Axis of Not So Much Evil Really as Just Generally Disagreeable...."

Inadvertantly attributed on the Internet to John Cleese Andrew Martlatt, American editor of Satirewire (b.1952)

A system built by the sweat of the many creates assassins to kill off the few. *Guns On The Roof.*
The Clash, British Rock Band

11

If we let people see that kind of thing, there would never again be any war. *Newsweek.*
> A Pentagon official on why footage of Iraqui soldiers sliced in two by helicopter fire was censored.

To be against war is not enough, it is hardly a beginning. And all things strive; we who try to speak know the ideas trying to be more human, we know things near their birth that try to become real. The truth here goes farther, there is another way of being against war and for poetry. We are against war and the sources of war. We are for poetry and the sources of poetry.
*The Life of Poetry,* (1949)
> Muriel Rukeyser, American Poet (1913–1980)

It's really not a number I'm terribly interested in.
> Response to the number of Iraqi people who were slaughtered by Americans in the 1991 "Desert Storm".
> Colin Powell, American Secetary of State (b.1937)

Who live under the shadow of a war.
What can I do that matters?
Who live under the Shadow.
> Stephen Spender, British Poet (1909-1995)

We do not have any defence treaties with Kuwait, and there are no special defence or security commitments to Kuwait.
> Said by Margaret Tutweiller, American State Department spokeswoman, 24th July 1990, nine days before Iraq's invasion of Kuwait

By God, we will make the fire eat up half of Israel if it tries to do anything against Iraq.
> Saddam Hussein, Iraqi President (b.1937)

The war won't ever be over... too damn profitable, do you get me? Back home they're coining money, the British are coining money; even the French, look at Bordeaux and Toulouse and Marseilles coining money and the goddam politicians, all of 'em got bank accounts in Amsterdam or Barcelona, the sons of bitches.
John Dos Passos, American Poet (1896–1970)

There are 13,000 strategic warheads, the United States then had 8,500. Russia's had decreased to about 10,000. France had 482, China 284, Britain 234. Israel was estimated to have 50 to 100; India had the capability for 80; and Pakistan owned 15 to 25. North Korea is believed to have had enough material for two to three bombs, and U.S authorities thought Iran was actively pursuing a secret program that would make it a nuclear power in about eight years. *Newsweek*, (1995)

In all wars the object is to protect or to seize money, property and power, and there will always be wars so long as Capital rules and oppresses people.
*War Against War.*
Ernst Friedrich, American Author (b.1924)

War is neither glamorous nor fun. There are no winners, only losers. There are no good wars, with the following exceptions: The American Revolution, World War II, and the Star Wars Trilogy. *Bart Simpson.*
From Bart The General, by John Swartzwelder

The guerrilla fights the war of the flea, and his military enemy suffers the dog's disadvantages: too much to defend; too small, ubiquitous, and agile an enemy to come to grips with. *The War of the Flea,* (2001)
Robert Taber, American Author (b.1944)

13

...70 percent of Serbia's military oil has gone; over half its usable aircraft have been destroyed; more than a fifth of the armoured units inside Kosovo are down; yesterday was the most successful allied day yet in hits on targets and artillery in Kosovo; and 40 percent of surface-to-air missiles have gone. There has been massive damage to Milosevic's infrastructure, but we must carry on and, if necessary, intensify. Parliament, May, 1999
Tony Blair, British Prime Minister (b.1953)

In Italy for thirty years under the Borgias they had warfare, terror, murder, bloodshed — they produced Michelangelo, Leonardo da Vinci and the Renaissance. In Switzerland they had brotherly love, five hundred years of democracy and peace and what did that produce? The cuckoo clock.
Orson Welles, American Film Director (1915-1985)

One hundred infidels commited suicide as they entered the holy city of Baghad. Their tanks will become their tombs.
Mohammed Saeed al-Sahaf, Iraqi Minister (b.1942)

... A spider web of 'patriots for profit', operating from the highest positions of special trust and confidence, have successfully circumvented our constitutional system in pursuit of a New World Order. They have infused America with drugs in order to fund covert operations while sealing the fate of our servicemen left in communist prisons.
James "Bo" Gritz, American Airforce Lt Col (b.1939)

You can no more win a war than you can win an earthquake.
Jeannette Rankin, American Pacifist (1880-1973)

We're not inflicting pain on these fuckers,' Clinton said, softly at first. 'When people kill us, they should be killed in greater numbers.' Then, with his face reddening, his voice rising, and his fist pounding his thigh, he leaned into Tony [Lake, then his national security adviser], as if it was his fault. 'I believe in killing people who try to hurt you.. And I can't believe we're being pushed around by these two-bit pricks.' *All Too Human*, (1999)
Ordering the bombing of civilian targets in Somalia, as told by, George Stephanopoulos
Bill Clinton, American President (b.1946)

We are effectively destroying ourselves by violence masquerading as love.
R.D. Laing, Scottish Pyschiatrist (1929-1989)

The U.S.A. has supplied arms, security equipment and training to governments and armed groups that have committed torture, political killings and other human rights abuses in countries around the world.
Amnesty International Report, October 1998.

War has been the most convenient pseudo-solution to the problems of twentieth-century capitalism. It provides the incentives to modernisation and technological revolution which the market and the pursuit of profit do only fitfully and by accident, it makes the unthinkable (such as votes for women and the abolition of unemployment) not merely thinkable but practicable ... What is equally important, it can re-create communities of men and give a temporary sense to their lives by uniting them against foreigners and outsiders. This is an achievement beyond the power of the private enterprise economy ... when left to itself.
Eric J. Hobsbawm, British Historian (b.1917)

Where is the indignation about the fact that the United States and Soviet Union have accumulated thirty thousand pounds of destructive force for every human being in the world?
Norman Cousins, American Author (1915-1990)

The pilot dropped the bomb in good faith, as you would expect of a trained pilot from a democratic NATO country to do.
Referring to NATO's bombing of Kosovar refugees
Jamie Shea, British Defense Minister (b.1953)

War should belong to the tragic past, to history: it should find no place on humanity's agenda for the future.
Pope John Paul II, Polish Pope (b.1920)

The day we executed the air campaign, I said, "we gotcha!"
Norman Schwarzkopf, American General (b.1934)

The real wars of religion are the wars religions unleash against ordinary citizens within their 'sphere of influence'
Salman Rushdie, Indian-born British Author (b.1947)

What we need is Star Peace and not Star Wars.
Mikhail S. Gorbachev, Russian Premier (b.1931)

The Libyan army is capable of destroying America and breaking its nose.
Muammar Qaddafi, Libyan Leader (b.1941)

War is capitalism with the gloves off. *Travesties*, (1975)
Tom Stoppard, Czech-born British Dramatist (b.1937)

16

Nuclear Armageddon At last, after innumerable glamorous and frightful years, mankind approaches a war which is totally predictable from beginning to end.
Frederic Raphael, American Author (b.1931)

I couldn't help but say to [Mr. Gorbachev], just think how easy his task and mine might be in these meetings that we held if suddenly there was a threat to this world from another planet. [We'd] find out once and for all that we really are all human beings here on this earth together.
Ronald Reagan, American President (b.1911)

War has become a luxury that only small nations can afford.
Hannah Arendt, German-born American Author (1906-1975)

Women have invented nothing in all that, except the men who were born as male babies and grew up to be men big enough to be killed fighting.
Janet Flanner, American Author (1892-1972)

Get up, stand up, stand up for your rights.
Get up, stand up, don't give up the fight.
*Get Up, Stand Up.* (1975)
Bob Marley, Jamaican Singer-songwriter (1945-1981)

Fighting. Men ... every man in the whole realm is in the army.... Every man in uniform ... An economy entirely geared to war ... but there is not much war ... hardly any fighting ... yet every man a soldier from birth till death ... Men ... all men for fighting ... but no war, no wars to fight ... what is it, what does it mean?
Doris Lessing, British Author (b.1919)

17

First World War Veterans slaughtered by General Eisenhower You give them your life, they give you a stab in the back Radiation, agent orange, tested on U.S. souls Guinea pigs for Western corporations I never have, I never will Pledge allegiance to their flag You're getting used, you'll end up dead.

Anti Flag, American Rock Band

Either war is obsolete or men are.

R. Buckminster Fuller, American Architect (1895-1983)

The draft is white people sending black people to fight yellow people to protect the country they stole from red people.

James Rado & Gerome Gragni, American Songwriters

You've got to forget about this civilian. Whenever you drop bombs, you're going to hit civilians.

Barry Goldwater, American Politician (1909-1998)

If it's natural to kill, how come men have to go into training to learn how?

Joan Baez, American Folk Singer (b.1941)

All my promises are lies, all my love is hate, I am the politician and I decide your fate. *Orgasmatron.*

Motorhead, British Rock Band

If the Nuremberg laws were applied, then every postwar American president would have been hanged.

Noam Chomsky, American Author (b.1928)

I'd like to see the government get out of war altogether and leave the whole feud to private industry. *Catch 22.*

Joseph Heller, American Author (b.1923)

18

We are at war with the most dangerous enemy that has ever faced mankind in his long climb from the swamp to the stars, and it has been said if we lose that war, and in so doing lose this way of freedom of ours, history will record with the greatest astonishment that those who had the most to lose did the least to prevent its happening.
> Ronald Reagan, American President (b.1911)

It is true we have won all our wars, but we have paid for them. We don't want victories anymore.
> Golda Meir, Israeli Prime Minister (1898-1978)

A visitor from Mars could easily pick out the civilized nations. They have the best implements of war.
> Herbert V. Prochnow, American Banker (1897-1998)

The great nations have always acted like gangsters, and the small nations like prostitutes.
> Stanley Kubrick, American Director (1928-1999)

When women are depressed they either eat or go shopping. Men invade another country.
> Elyane Boosler, American Comedian (b.1952)

[John] Dalton's records, carefully preserved for a century, were destroyed during the World War II bombing of Manchester. It is not only the living who are killed in war.
> John Dalton was a renowed English Chemist
> Isaac Asimov, American Author (1920-1992)

What is it good for? Absolutely Nothing!!
> Edwin Starr, Barret Strong & Norman Whitfield

Draft beer; not people.
> Author Unknown

Mr. President, have you approved of covert activity to destablise the present government of Nicaragua? A. "Well, no, we're supporting them, the — oh, wait a minute, wait a minute, I'm sorry, I was thinking of El Salvador, because of the previous, when you said Nicaragua. Here again, this is something upon which the national security interests, I just — I will not comment".

> As quoted by John Pilger in *Heroes* (1986)
> Ronald Reagan, American President (b.1911)

What good does it do to ban some guns. All guns should be banned.

> Howard Metzanbaum, American Politician (b.1917)

We want a world free of war, without arms races, nuclear weapons and violence.

> Mikhail S. Gorbachev, Russian Premier (b.1931)

War is for everyone, for children too.
I wasn't going to tell you and I mustn't.
The best way is to come uphill with me
And have our fire and laugh and be afraid.
*The Bonfire.*

> Robert Frost, American Poet (1874–1963)

The neutron warhead is a defensive weapon designed to offset the great superiority that the Soviet Union has on the western front against the NATO nations.

> Ronald Reagan, American President (b.1911)

While maintaining our nuclear potential at the proper level, we need to devote more attention to developing the entire range of means of information warfare.

> Boris Yeltsin, Russian Premier (b.1931)

A world without nuclear weapons would be less stable and more dangerous for all of us.
Margaret Thatcher, British Prime Minister (b.1925)

In a war of ideas it is people who get killed.
Stanislaw J. Lec, Polish Author (1909-1966)

Has anybody here seen my old friend Abraham, can you tell me where he's gone? He freed a lot of people, but it seems the good they die young.
*Abraham, Martin, and John.*
Dion Demucii, American Singer-songwriter

In an incredible perversion of justice, former soldiers who sprayed festeringly poisonous chemicals on Vietnam, and now find today that they themselves have been damaged by them, appeal to the people for sympathy and charity. The effects of the defoliant "Agent Orange" are discussed at length, but not one single newspaper article or hearing that we are aware of has even mentioned the effects of the people who still live in those regions of Vietnam. It's as outlandish as if Nazis who gassed Jews were now to come forward and whine that the poisons they utilized had finally made *them* sick.The staggering monstrousness goes unlaughed at and even unnoticed, as in a Kafka novel.*The Match*, No 79.
Fred Woodworth, American Anarchist (b.1946)

Dead battles, like dead generals, hold the military mind in their dead grip. *August 1914* (1962)
Babara W. Tuchman, American Author (1912-1989)

I'm neither left or right. I'm just staying home tonight, getting lost in that hopeless little screen. *Democracy*
Leonard Cohen, Canadian Singer-songwriter (b.1934)

The aim of military training is not just to prepare men for battle, but to make them long for it.
Louis Simpson, Jamaican Poet (b.1923)

I'm old and crazy, but I still give a damn. And I still think the boys got screwed over in Vietnam. *G.I. Joe.*
Waylon Jennings, American Singer-songwriter (1937-2002)

Saigon was an addicted city, and we were the drug: the corruption of children, the mutilation of young men, the prostitution of women, the humiliation of the old, the division of the family, the division of the country — it had all been done in our name ... The French city ... had represented the opium stage of the addiction. With the Americans had begun the heroin phase.
James Fenton, British Author (b.1949)

Sometime they'll give a war and nobody will come.
Carl Sandburg, American Poet (1878-1967)

We should declare war on North Vietnam ... We could pave the whole country and put parking strips on it, and still be home by Christmas.
Ronald Reagan, American President (b.1911)

Television brought the brutality of war into the comfort of the living room. Vietnam was lost in the living rooms of America — not on the battlefields of Vietnam.
*Montreal Gazette*, (1975)
Marshall McLuhan, Canadian Philosopher (1911-1981)

Gentlemen, you can't fight in here... This is the War Room! From *Dr. Strangelove*, (1964)
Peter Sellers, British Actor (1925-1980)

No country can act wisely simultaneously in every part of the globe at every moment of time.

Henry Kissinger, German-born American Diplomat
(b.1923)

We have no honorable intentions in Vietnam. Our minimal expectation is to occupy it as an American colony and maintain social stability for our investments. This tells why American helicopters are being used against guerrillas in Colombia and Peru. Increasingly the role our nation has taken is the role of those who refuse to give up the privileges and pleasures that come from the immense profits of overseas investment.

Speech given at Riverside Church New York City,1974
Martin Luther King Jr, American Civil Rights Leader
(1929-1968)

The military don't start wars. The politicians start wars.

William Westmorland, American General (b.1914)

War can only be abolished through war, and in order to get rid of the gun it is necessary to take up the gun.
*Problems of War and Strategy.*

Mao Tse-Tung, Chinese Chairman (1893–1976)

War grows out of the desire of the individual to gain advantage at the expense of his fellow man.

Napoleon Hill, American Author (1883-1970)

The attack on Yugoslavia constitutes the most brazen international aggression since the Nazis attacked Poland to prevent "Polish atrocities" against Germans.
*Chicago Tribune.*

Walter J. Rockler, American Lawyer (1921-2003)

It takes two to make war.
> John F. Kennedy, American President (1917-1963)

Asia's crowded and Europe's too old, Africa is far too hot and Canada's too cold. And South America stole our name, let's drop the big one. *Political Science.*
> Randy Newman, American Singer-songwriter (b.1943)

Our scientific power has outrun our spiritual power. We have guided missiles and misguided men.
*Strength to Love*, (1963)
> Martin Luther King Jr, American Civil Rights Leader (1929-1968)

A revolution is not a dinner party, or writing an essay, or painting a picture, or doing embroidery; it cannot be so refined, so leisurely and gentle, so temperate, kind, courteous, restrained and magnanimous. A revolution is an insurrection, an act of violence by which one class overthrows another.
> Mao Tse-Tung, Chinese Chairman (1893–1976)

Violence is the first refuge of the incompetent
> Isaac Asimov, American Author (1920-1992)

They wrote in the old days that it is sweet and fitting to die for one's country. But in modern war, there is nothing sweet nor fitting in your dying. You will die like a dog for no good reason.
> Ernest Hemingway, American Author (1899-1961)

Men love war because it allows them to look serious. Because it is the one thing that stops women laughing at them. *The Magus*, (1965)
> John Fowles, British Author (b.1926)

The U.S. has broken the second rule of war. That is, don't go fighting with your land army on the mainland of Asia. Rule One is don't march on Moscow. I developed these two rules myself.

Referring to the Vietnam War
Bernard Law Montgomery, British Field Marshal
(1887–1976)

We sent Marines into Lebanon and you only have to go to Lebanon, to Syria or to Jordan to witness first-hand the intense hatred among many people for the United States because we bombed and shelled and unmercifully killed totally innocent villagers — women and children and farmers and housewives — in those villages around Beirut. As a result of that... we became kind of a Satan in the minds of those who are deeply resentful. That is what precipitated the taking of our hostages and that is what has precipitated some of the terrorist attacks.

Jimmy Carter, American President (b.1924)

Never think that war, no matter how necessary, nor how justified, is not a crime.

Ernest Hemingway, American Author (1899-1961)

No event in American history is more misunderstood than the Vietnam War. It was misreported then, and it is misremembered now.

Richard M. Nixon, American President (1913-1994)

I have never understood this liking for war. It panders to instincts already catered for within the scope of any respectable domestic establishment.
*Forty Years On*, (1968)

Alan Bennett, British Playwright (b.1934)

It is not enough to say; We must not wage war.
Martin Luther King Jr, American Civil Rights Leader
(1929-1968)

When the enemy advances, withdraw; when he stops, harass; when he tires, strike; when he retreats, pursue.
Mao Tse-Tung, Chinese Chairman (1893-1976)

To win in Vietnam, we will have to exterminate a nation.
*Dr Spock on Vietnam,* (1968)

Dr. Benjamin Spock,
American Author
(1903-1998)

I'm fed up to the ears with old men dreaming up wars for young men to die in.
George McGovern,
American Politician
(b.1922)

The guns and the bombs, the rockets and the warships, are all symbols of human failure.
Lyndon B. Johnson, American President (1908-1973)

Will... the threat of common extermination continue? Must children receive the arms race from us as a necessary inheritance?
Speech at the UN in 1979
John Paul II, Polish Pope (b.1920)

There were so many people killed that day it is hard for me to recall exactly how some of the people died.
Referring to the My Lai massace
Varnado Simpson, American Army Private

Mankind must put an end to war, or war will put an end to mankind.
> John F. Kennedy, American President (1917-1963)

Have we not come to such an impasse in the modern world that we must love our enemies — or else? The chain reaction of evil — hate begetting hate, wars producing more wars — must be broken, or else we shall be plunged into the dark abyss of annihilation.
> Martin Luther King Jr, American Civil Rights Leader
> (1929-1968)

You will kill ten of our men, and we will kill one of yours, and in the end it will be you who tire of it.
> Ho Chi Minh, North Vietnamese Leader (1890-1969)

War is the continuation of politics'. In this sense war is politics and war itself is a political action.
*Quotations from Chairman Mao Tse-Tung.*
> Mao Tse-Tung, Chinese Chairman (1893-1976)

I'd like to explain why you fine young men had to be blown apart to defend this mud hole.
*Song For The Dead.*
> Randy Newman, American Singer-songwriter (b.1943)

Revolution is bloody, revolution is hostile, revolution knows no compromise, and revolution overturns and destroys everything that gets in its way.
> Malcolm X, American Muslim Leader (1925-1965)

The conventional army loses if it does not win. The guerrilla wins if he does not lose.
*The Vietnam Negotiations*, (1969)
> Henry Kissinger, German-born American Diplomat
> (b.1923)

27

The war was won on both sides: by the Vietnamese on the ground, by the Americans in the electronic mental space. And if the one side won an ideological and political victory, the other made Apocalypse Now and that has gone right around the world. *Astral America,* (1986)
Jean Baudrillard, French Semiologist (b.1929)

The real trouble with (modern war) is that it gives no one a chance to kill the right people.
Ezra Pound, American Poet (1885-1972)

I'm for peace — I've yet to see a man wake up in the morning and say, I've just had a good war.
Mae West, American Film Actress (1893-1980)

The most persistent sound which reverberates through men's history is the beating of war drums.
*Janus: A Summing Up,* (1979)
Arthur Koestler, Hungarian-born British Author
(1905-1983)

The more bombers, the less room for doves of peace.
Nikita S. Khrushchev, Russian Premier (1894-1971)

Mummy do you think there'll drop the bomb.
*The Wall.* (1979)
Roger Waters, British Singer-songwriter (b.1944)

Men like war: they do not hold much sway over birth, so they make up for it with death. Unlike women, men menstruate by shedding other people's blood.
Lucy Ellman, American Author (b.1956)

When you can whip any man in the world, you never know peace.
Muhammad Ali, American Boxer (b.1942)

In an all-out nuclear war, more destructive power than in all of World War II would be unleashed every second during the long afternoon it would take for all the missiles and bombs to fall. A World War II every second — more people killed in the first few hours than all the wars of history put together. The survivors, if any, would live in despair amid the poisoned ruins of a civilization that had committed suicide.

Jimmy Carter, American President (b.1924)

Military intelligence is a contradiction in terms.

Groucho Marx, American Comedian (1890-1977)

War-making is one of the few activities that people are not supposed to view "realistically"; that is, with an eye to expense and practical outcome. In all-out war, expenditure is all-out, unprudent — war being defined as an emergency in which no sacrifice is excessive.

Susan Sontag, American Author (b.1933)

We are advocates of the abolition of war, we do not want war; but war can only be abolished through war, and in order to get rid of the gun it is necessary to take up the gun. *Quotations from Chairman Mao Tse-Tung.*

Mao Tse-Tung, Chinese Chairman (1893-1976)

No more war! Never again war! If you wish to be brothers, drop your weapons.

Paul VI, Italian Pope (1897-1978)

When the rich wage war, it's the poor who die.

Jean-Paul Sartre, French Philospher (1905-1980)

Revolution is the festival of the oppressed

Germaine Greer, Australian Author (b.1939)

I was proud of the youths who opposed the war in Vietnam because they were my babies.
Dr. Benjamin Spock, American Author (1903-1998)

In the long term we can hope that religion will change the nature of man and reduce conflict. But history is not encouraging in this respect. The bloodiest wars in history have been religious wars.
Richard M. Nixon, American President (1913-1994)

Power comes not from the barrel of a gun, but from one's awareness of his or her own cultural strength and the unlimited capacity to empathize with, feel for, care, and love one's brothers and sisters.
Addison Gayle, Jr, American Educator (b.1932)

By jove, no wonder women don't love war nor understand it, nor can operate in it as a rule; it takes a man to suffer what other men have invented.
Janet Flanner, American Author (1892-1972)

If the Americans do not want to support us anymore, let them go, get out! Let them forget their humanitarian promises!
Nguyen Van Thieu, South Vietnamese President (1923-2001)

We are not about to send American boys nine or ten thousand miles away from home to do what Asian boys ought to be doing for themselves.
Lyndon B. Johnson, American President (1908-1973)

We have met the enemy and he is us.
Walt Kelly, American Cartoonist (1913-1973)

The bomb that fell on Hiroshima fell on America too. It fell on no city, no munition plants, no docks. It erased no church, vaporized no public buildings, reduced no man to his atomic elements. But it fell, it fell.
*The Bomb That Fell on America.*
Hermann Hagedorn, American Poet (1882-1964)

It seems like such a terrible shame that innocent civilians have to get hurt in wars, otherwise combat would be such a wonderfully healthy way to rid the human race of unneeded trash.
Fred Woodworth, American Anarcist (b.1946)

You're an old-timer if you can remember when setting the world on fire was a figure of speech.
Referring to the Atomic bomb
Franklin P. Jones, American Businessman (1887-1929)

I will not play tug o' war. I'd rather play hug o' war. Where everyone hugs instead of tugs, Where everyone giggles and rolls on the rug, Where everyone kisses, and everyone grins, and everyone cuddles, and everyone wins.
Shel Silverstein, American Poet (1930-1999)

One of the greatest casualties of the war in Vietnam is the Great Society ... shot down on the battlefield of Vietnam.
Martin Luther King Jr, American Civil Rights Leader
(1929-1968)

"Once the rockets are up, who cares where they come down? That's not my department,"says Wernher von Braun.*Wernher Braun* (1965)
Tom Lehrer, American singer-songwriter (b.1928)

There's a graveyard in northern France where all the dead boys from D-Day are buried. The white crosses reach from one horizon to the other. I remember looking it over and thinking it was a forest of graves. But the rows were like this, dizzying, diagonal, perfectly straight, so after all it wasn't a forest but an orchard of graves. Nothing to do with nature, unless you count human nature. *Animal Dreams*, (1991)
> Barbara Kingsolver, American Author (b.1955)

In modern war... you will die like a dog for no good reason.
> Ernest Hemingway, American Author (1899-1961)

The expendability factor has increased by being transferred from the specialised, scarce and expensively trained military personnel to the amorphous civilian population. American strategists have calculated the proportion of civilians killed in this century's major wars. In the First World War 5 per cent of those killed were civilians, in the Second World War 48 per cent, while in a Third World War 90-95 per cent would be civilians. *Anarchy in Action.*
> Colin Ward, British Author (b.1924)

Borders are scratched across the hearts of men
By strangers with a calm, judicial pen,
And when the borders bleed we watch with dread
The lines of ink across the map turn red.
*Rhymes for Our Times*, (1959)
> Marya Mannes, American Author (1904-1990)

If I had a rocket launcher. *Stealing Fire*, (1984)
> Bruce Coburn, Canadian Singer-songwriter (b.1948)

Today the real test of power is not capacity to make war but capacity to prevent it.
Anne O'Hare McCormick, American Author(1880-1954)

Everyone's a pacifist between wars. It's like being a vegetarian between meals.
Colman McCarthy, American Peace Activist (b.1938)

War will exist until that distant day when the conscientious objector enjoys the same reputation and prestige that the warrior does today.
John F. Kennedy, American President (1917-1963)

I began revolution with 82 men. If I had to do it again, I'd do it with 10 or 15 and absolute faith. It does not matter how small you are if you have faith and plan of action.
Fidel Castro, Cuban President (b.1926)

Kill a man and you're a murderer, kill many and you're a conqueror. *Captive Honor.*
Megadeth, American Rock Band

We have war when at least one of the parties to a conflict wants something more than it wants peace.
Jeane J. Kirkpatrick, American Diplomat (b.1926)

I have no doubt that we will be successful in harnessing the sun's energy ... If sunbeams were weapons of war, we would have had solar energy centuries ago.
Sir George Porter, British Chemist (b.1920)

War is fear cloaked in courage.
William Westmorland, American General (b.1914)

We kill because we are afraid of our own shadow, afraid that if we used a little common sense we'd have to admit that our glorious principles were wrong.
*The Wisdom of the Heart,* (1941)
Henry Miller, American Author (1891-1980)

I would like it if men had to partake in the same hormonal cycles to which we're subjected monthly. Maybe that's why men declare war — because they have a need to bleed on a regular basis.
Brett Butler, American Comedian (b.1982)

Vietnam was the first war ever fought without any censorship. Without censorship, things can get terribly confused in the public mind.
William Westmorland, American General (b.1914)

Wars usually have the effect of speeding up the process of history. *Debates With Historians.*
Pieter Geyl, Dutch Author (1887-1966)

Men were made for war. Without it they wandered greyly about, getting under the feet of the women, who were trying to organize the really important things of life.
Alice Thomas Ellis, British Author (b.1932)

Why do we kill people who are killing people to show that killing people is wrong?
Holly Near, American Musician (b1949)

War is the only game in which it doesn't pay to have the home-court advantage.
Dick Motta, American Sports Coach (b1942)

If we lose this war, I'll start another in my wife's name.
Moshe Dayan, Israeli General (1915-1981)

The tragedy of war is that it uses man's best to do man's worst.

> Henry Fosdick, American Teacher

I think war might be God's way of teaching us geography.

> Paul Rodriguez, American Comedian (b.1958)

Are bombs the only way of setting fire to the spirit of a people? Is the human will as inert as the past two world-wide wars would indicate?

> Gregory Clark, British Author (b.1936)

The wrong war, at the wrong place, at the wrong time, and with the wrong enemy.

> Against the Korean war expanding into China in 1951
> Omar Nelson Bradley, American General (1893-1981)

The basic problems facing the world today are not susceptible to a military solution.

> John F. Kennedy, American President (1917-1963)

I shouted out who killed the Kennedys, when after all it was you and me. *Sympathy For The Devil.*

> The Rolling Stones, British Rock Band

No one has ever succeeded in keeping nations at war except by lies.

> Salvador de Madariaga, Spanish Author (1886-1978)

The ultimate decision about what is accepted as right and wrong will be made not by individual human wisdom but by the disappearance of the groups that have adhered to the "wrong" beliefs.

> Friedrich A. Hayek, Austrian Philosopher (1899-1992)

War creates no absolutely new situation: it simply aggravates the permanent human situation so that we can no longer ignore it. Human life has always been lived on the edge of a precipice.

C. S Lewis, British Author (1898-1963)

Lots of people who complained about us receiving the MBE received theirs for heroism in the war — for killing people. We received ours for entertaining other people. I'd say we deserve ours more.

John Lennon, British Singer-songwriter (1940-1980)

I said, I'm gonna buy a gun and start a war. If you can tell me something worth fighting for.
*A Rush Of Blood To The Head.* (2002)

Coldplay, British Rock Band

I have talked to old men who were on the battlefield at that last moment (Armistice).They have told me in one way or another that the sudden silence was the Voice of God.*The Breakfast of Champions*, (1961)

Kurt Vonnegut, American Author (b.1928)

Once and for all the idea of glorious victories won by the glorious army must be wiped out. Neither side is glorious. On either side they're just frightened men messing their pants and they all want the same thing — not to lie under the earth, but to walk upon it — without crutches.

Peter Weiss, German Author (1916-1982)

There are no atheists in foxholes isn't an argument against atheism, it's an argument against foxholes.

James Morrow, American Author (b.1947)

War will exist until that distant day when the conscientious objector enjoys the same reputation and prestige that the warrior does today.
John F. Kennedy, American President (1917-1963)

In war, there are no unwounded soldiers.
José Narosky, French-born Argentinian (1892-1924)

Three things strengthen a nation's defenses: gentleness, justice and generosity.
Arab proverb

There's a time past I thought guns shoot death. But now that I bury by the day, I see guns shoot fear. And I know also the words 'Forgive them Lord, they know not what they do.
Sipho Sepamla, South African Poet

A "just war" is hospitable to every self-deception on the part of those waging it, none more than the certainty of virtue, under whose shelter every abomination can be committed with a clear conscience.
Alexander Cockburn, Irish-born American Journalist (b.1941)

I know war as few other men now living know it, and nothing to me is more revolting. I have long advocated its complete abolition, as its very destructiveness on both friend and foe has rendered it useless as a method of settling international disputes.
Ernest Hemingway, American Author (1899-1961)

Every revolutionary ends up either by becoming an oppressor or a heretic.
Albert Camus, French Author (1913-1962)

Mankind has grown strong in eternal struggles and it will only perish through eternal peace
Adolf Hitler, German Chancellor (1889-1945)

The War of the Roses in England and the Civil War in America were both intestinal conflicts arising out of similar ideas. In the first the clash was between feudalism and the new economic order; in the second, between an agricultural society and a new industrial one. Both led to similar ends; the first to the founding of the English nation, and the second to the founding of the American.Both were strangely interlinked; for it was men of the old military and not of the new economic mind — men, such as Sir Humphrey Gilbert and Sir Walter Raleigh — who founded the English colonies in America.
J.F.C. Fuller, British Historian (1878–1966)

Those who have long enjoyed such privileges as we enjoy forget in time that men have died to win them.
Franklin D. Roosevelt, American President (1882-1945)

I've got to go to meet God — and explain all those men I killed at Alamein.
Bernard Law Montgomery, British Field Marshal (1887–1976)

Don't fight a battle if you don't gain anything by winning.
Erwin Rommel, German General (1891-1944)

Nations have recently been led to borrow billions for war; no nation has ever borrowed largely for education. Probably, no nation is rich enough to pay for both war and civilization. We must make our choice; we cannot have both.

Abraham Flexner, American Author (1866-1959)

War is, at first, the hope that one will be better off; next, the expectation that the other fellow will be worse off; then, the satisfaction that he isn't any better off; and, finally, the surprise at everyone's being worse off.

Karl Kraus, Austrian Author (1874-1936)

In war, whichever side may call itself the victor, there are no winners, but all are losers.

Neville Chamberlain, British Prime Minister (1869-1940)

Wars, conflict, it's all business. One murder makes a villain. Millions a hero. Numbers sanctify.

*Monsieur Verdoux*, (1947)

Charlie Chaplin, British-born American Film Actor (1889-1977)

The redress of the grievances of the vanquished should precede the disarmament of the victors.

*The Gathering Storm*, (1948)

Sir Winston Churchill, British Prime Minister(1874-1965)

Older men declare war. But it is youth that must fight and die.

Herbert Hoover, American President (1874-1964)

War is only a cowardly escape from the problems of peace.

Thomas Mann, German Author (1875-1955)

To delight in war is a merit in the soldier, a dangerous quality in the captain, and a positive crime in the statesman.
George Santayana, Spanish-born American Philosopher (1863-1952)

The release of atom power has changed everything except our way of thinking... the solution to this problem lies in the heart of mankind. If only I had known, I should have become a watchmaker.
Albert Einstein, German-born American Physicist (1879-1955)

War is war. The only good human being is a dead one.
*Animal Farm*, (1945)
George Orwell, British Author (1903-1950)

Traditional nationalism cannot survive the fissioning of the atom. One world or none.
Stuart Chase, American Author (1888-1995)

A single death is a tragedy, a million deaths is a statistic.
Comment to Churchill at Potsdam, in 1945
Joseph Stalin, Russian Premier (1879-1953)

What is a war criminal? Was not war itself a crime against God and humanity, and, therefore, were not all those who sanctioned, engineered, and conducted wars, war criminals? War criminals are not confined to the Axis Powers alone. Roosevelt and Churchill are no less war criminals than Hitler and Mussolini. England, America and Russia have all of them got their hands dyed more or less red — not merely Germany and Japan.
Mahatma Gandhi, Indian Political Leader (1869-1948)

War on the destiny of man!
Doom on the sun!
Before death takes you, O take back this.
*Find meat on bones.*
Dylan Thomas, Welsh Poet (1914–1953)

In the arts of life man invents nothing; but in the arts of death he outdoes Nature herself, and produces by chemistry and machinery all the slaughter of plague, pestilence and famine.
George Bernard Shaw, Irish Author (1856-1950)

The object of war is not to die for your country but to make the other bastard die for his.
George S. Patton, American General (1885-1945)

Hitler and Mussolini were only the primary spokesmen for the attitude of domination and craving for power that are in the heart of almost everyone. Until the source is cleared, there will always be confusion and hate, wars and class antagonisms.
J. Krishnamurti, Indian Philosopher (1895-1986)

Naturally, the common people don't want war ... but after all it is the leaders of a country who determine the policy, and it is always a simple matter to drag the people along, whether it is a democracy, or a fascist dictatorship, or a parliament, or a communist dictatorship.Voice or no voice, the people can always be brought to the bidding of the leaders. That is easy. All you have to do is to tell them they are being attacked, and denounce the pacifists for lack of patriotism and exposing the country to danger. It works the same in every country.
Hermann Goering, German General (1893-1946)

I said that the world must be made safe for at least fifty years. If it was only for fifteen to twenty years then we should have betrayed our soldiers.
*Closing the Ring*, (1951)
Sir Winston Churchill, British Prime Minister(1874-1965)

One is left with the horrible feeling now that war settles nothing; that to win a war is as disastrous as to lose one.*Autobiography*, (1977)
Agatha Christie, British Author (1890-1976)

We've been looking for the enemy for several days now, we've finally found them. We're surrounded. That simplifies our problem of getting to these people and killing them.
Lewis B. "Chesty" Puller, American LtGen (1898-1971)

Duty, honor, country: Those three hallowed words reverently dictate what you ought to be, what you can be, what you will be. They are your rallying point to build courage when courage seems to fail, to regain faith when there seems to be little cause for faith, to create hope when hope becomes forlorn.... In my dreams I hear again the crash of guns, the rattle of musketry, the strange, mournful mutter of the battlefield. But in the evening of my memory always I come back to West Point. Always there echoes and re-echoes: Duty, honor, country.
Douglas MacArthur, American General (1880-1964)

Ladies and gentlemen, there is no more profitable course of action, than to go to war with the United States and lose!
Prime Minister Montjoy, In *The Mouse That Roared*, (1961)

In starting and waging a war it is not right that matters, but victory. *The Rise and Fall of the Third Reich.*(1992)
By William L. Shirer
Adolf Hitler, German Chancellor (1889-1945)

I always thought I was Jeanne d'Arc and Napoleon Bonaparte. How little one knows oneself.
His reply when compared to Robespierre
Charles de Gaulle, French President (1890-1970)

The war shook down the Tsardom, an unspeakable abomination, and made an end of the new German Empire and the old Apostolic Austrian one. It ... gave votes and seats in Parliament to women... But if society can be reformed only by the accidental results of horrible catastrophes ... what hope is there for mankind in them? The war was a horror and everybody is the worse for it.
George Bernard Shaw, Irish Playwright, (1856–1950)

I hate war as only a soldier who has lived it can, only as one who has seen its brutality, its futility, its stupidity.
Dwight D. Eisenhower, American President (1890-1969)

We shall defend our island, whatever the cost may be, we shall fight on the beaches, we shall fight on the landing grounds, we shall fight in the fields and in the streets, we shall fight in the hills; we shall never surrender.
Sir Winston Churchill, British Prime Minister(1874-1965)

War will never cease until babies begin to come into the world with larger cerebrums and smaller adrenal glands.
H.L Mencken, American Author (1880-1956)

The graveyards are full of indispensable men.
Charles de Gaulle, French President (1890-1970)

43

The first casualty when war comes is truth.
Hiram Johnson, American Politician (1888-1945)

The war has developed not necessarily to Japan's advantage.
Hirohito, Japanese Emperor (1901-1989)

The atomic bomb made the prospect of future war unendurable. It has led us up those last few steps to the mountain pass; and beyond there is a different country.
Robert Oppenheimer, American Physicist (1904-1967)

More than an end to war, we want an end to the beginnings of all wars.
Franklin D. Roosevelt, American President (1882-1945)

The eyes of the world are upon you. The hopes and prayers of liberty-loving people everywhere march with you.
Address to his troops on D-Day, 1944
Dwight D. Eisenhower, American President (1890-1969)

People sleep peaceably in their beds at night only because rough men stand ready to do violence on their behalf.
George Orwell, British Author (1903-1940)

Patriotism is the willingness to kill and be killed for trivial reasons.
Bertrand Russell, British Philosopher (1872-1970)

Success is how high you bounce when you hit bottom.
George S. Patton, America General (1885-1945)

A man can be destroyed but not defeated.
Ernest Hemingway, American Author (1899-1961)

We are not retreating — we are advancing in another direction.
Douglas MacArthur, American General (1880-1964)

Guns will make us powerful; butter will only make us fat.
Hermann Goering, German General (1893-1946)

What difference does it make to the dead, the orphans, and the homeless, whether the mad destruction is wrought under the name of totalitarianism or the holy name of liberty and democracy?
Mahatma Gandhi, Indian Political Leader (1869-1948)

Men are at war with each other because each man is at war with himself.
Francis Meehan, British Chemist (1898-1957)

The British soldier can stand up to anything except the British War Office. *The Devil's Disciple*, (1897)
George Bernard Shaw, Irish Author (1856-1950)

Men will not fight and die without knowing what they are fighting and dying for.
Douglas MacArthur, American General (1880-1964)

War is to man what maternity is to a woman. From a philosophical and doctrinal viewpoint, I do not believe in perpetual peace.
Benito Mussolini, Italian Prime Minister (1883-1945)

Generals think war should be waged like the tourneys of the Middle Ages. I have no use for knights; I need revolutionaries.
Adolf Hitler, German Chancellor (1889-1945)

To save your world you asked this man to die: Would this man, could he see you now, ask why?
*Epitaph for an Unknown Soldier.* (1922)
W. H. Auden, British Poet (1907-1973)

The problem in defense is how far you can go without destroying from within what you are trying to defend from without.
Dwight D. Eisenhower, American President (1890-1969)

Youth is the first victim of war; the first fruit of peace. It takes 20 years or more of peace to make a man; it takes only 20 seconds of war to destroy him.
Baudouin I, King of Belgium (1930-1993)

There never has been a war yet which, if the facts had been put calmly before the ordinary folk, could not have been prevented. The common man I think, is the great protection against war.
Ernest Bevin, British Politcian (1881-1951)

Oh war! war! the dream of patriots and heroes. A fraud. Bluntschli, a hollow sham. *Arms and the Man,* (1894)
Gerorge Bernard Shaw, Irish Author (1856-1950)

The way to win an atomic war is to make certain it never starts.
Omar Bradley, American General (1893-1981)

The world has achieved brilliance without wisdom, power without conscience. Ours is a world of nuclear giants and ethical infants. We know more about war than we know about peace, more about killing than we know about living.
Omar Bradley, American General (1893-1981)

If it were proved to me that in making war, my ideal had a chance of being realized, I would still say "no" to war. For one does not create a human society on mounds of corpses.

> Louis Lecoin, French Author (1888-1971)

Fighting is like champagne. It goes to the heads of cowards as quickly as of heroes. Any fool can be brave on a battle field when it's be brave or else be killed.
*Gone with the Wind*, (1936)

> Margaret Mitchell, American Author (1909-1949)

When you are winning a war almost everything that happens can be claimed to be right and wise.

> Sir Winston Churchill, British Prime Minister(1874-1965)

War is peace. Freedom is slavery. Ignorance is strength.

> George Orwell, British Author (1903-1950)

Love is like war: easy to begin but very hard to stop.

> H.L Mencken, American Author (1880-1956)

That's what you are. That's what you all are. All of you young people who served in the war. You are a lost generation. *A Moveable Feast*, (1926)

> Gertrude Stein, American Author (1874-1946)

The only winner in the War of 1812 was Tchaikovsky.

> Sloman Short

In a civil war, a general must know — and I'm afraid it's a thing rather of instinct than of practice — he must know exactly when to move over to the other side. *Not a Drum was Heard: The War Memoirs of General Gland.*

> Henry Reed, British Poet (1914-1986)

If we don't end war, war will end us.
*Things to Come*, (1935)
H.G. Wells, British Author (1866-1946)

And I can fight only for something that I love, love only what I respect, and respect only what I at least know.
*Mein Kampf.* (1924)
Adolf Hitler, German Chancellor (1889-1945)

War is not an adventure. It is a disease. It is like typhus.
Antoine de Saint-Exupery, French Author (1900-1944)

Like German opera, too long and too loud.
His opinion after the Battle of Crete,1941.
Evelyn Waugh, British Author (1903-1966)

War does not determine who is right—only who is left.
Bertrand Russell, British Philosopher (1872-1970)

Studies by Medical Corps psychiatrists of combat fatigue cases... found that fear of killing, rather than fear of being killed, was the most common cause of battle failure, and that fear of failure ran a strong second.
S.L.A. Marshall, American Author (1900-1977)

You can't say civilization isn't advancing: in every war, they kill you in a new way.
Will Rogers, American Humorist (1879-1934)

The release of atom power has changed everything except our way of thinking... the solution to this problem lies in the heart of mankind. If only I had known, I should have become a watchmaker.
Albert Einstein, German-born American Physicist
(1879-1955)

Praise the Lord and pass the ammunition!
> At the Japanese attack on Pearl Harbor, Dec 1941.
> Howell M. Forgy, American Naval Chaplain (1908-1983)

There is nothing that war has ever achieved that we could not better achieve without it.
> Henry Havelock Ellis, English Psychologist (1859-1939)

The ability and inclination to use physical strength is no indication of bravery or tenacity to life. The greatest cowards are often the greatest bullies. Nothing is cheaper and more common than physical bravery. *Resist Not Evil.*
> Clarence Darrow, American Lawyer (1857-1938)

In war there is no substitute for victory.
> Douglas MacArthur, American General (1880-1964)

This marvelous force of Life of which you boast is a force of Death: Man measures his strength by his destructiveness. What is his religion? An excuse for hating me. What is his law? An excuse for hanging you. What is his morality? Gentility! An excuse for consuming without producing. What is his art? An excuse for gloating over pictures of slaughter. What are his politics? Either the worship of a despot because a despot can kill, or parliamentary cockfighting.
*Man and Superman,* (1903)
> George Bernard Shaw, Irish Author (1856-1950)

Wars have never hurt anybody except the people who die.
> Salvador Dali, Spanish Painter (1904-1989)

Anyone, who truly wants to go to war, has never truly been there before!
> Larry Reeves

We knew the world could not be the same. A few people laughed, a few people cried. Most people were silent. I remembered the line from the Hindu scripture, the *Bhagavad Gita*: "I am became Death, the destroyers of worlds." I suppose we all thought that, one way or another.
Robert Oppenheimer, American Physicist (1904-1967)

How vile and despicable war seems to me! I would rather be hacked in pieces than take part in such an abominable business. *Ideas and Opinions,* (1954)
Albert Einstein, German-born American
Physicist (1879-1955)

Most people would rather die than think and most do.
Bertrand Russell, British Philosopher (1872-1970)

We must become the owners, or at any rate the controllers at the source, of at least a proportion of the oil which we require.
British Royal Commission, agreeing with Winston
Churchill's policy towards Iraq in 1913.

In the councils of government, we must guard against the acquisition of unwarranted influence, whether sought or unsought, by the military industrial complex. The potential for the disastrous rise of misplaced power exists and will persist.
Dwight D. Eisenhower, American President (1890-1969)

Jaw-jaw is better than war-war.
Harold MacMillan, British Prime Minister (1894-1986)

Old soldiers never die; they just fade away.
Douglas MacArthur, American General (1880-1964)

War stirs in men's hearts the mud of their worst instincts. It puts a premium on violence, nourishes hatred, and gives free rein to cupidity. It crushes the weak, exalts the unworthy, and bolsters tyranny...Time and time again it has destroyed all ordered living, devastated hope, and put the prophets to death.
Charles de Gaulle, French President (1890-1970)

Diplomats are just as essential in starting a war as soldiers are in finishing it.
Will Rogers, American Humorist (1879-1935)

We Germans have a far greater and more urgent duty towards civilization to perform than the Great Asiatic Power. We, like the Japanese, can only fulfil it by the sword. *Germany and the Next War*, (1914)
Friedrich von Bernhardi, German Author (1849-1930)

The release of atomic energy has not created a new problem. It has merely made more urgent the necessity of solving an existing one. *Atomic War or Peace.*
Albert Einstein, German-born American Physicist (1879-1955)

We are going to have peace even if we have to fight for it.
Dwight D. Eisenhower, American President (1890-1969)

War is a biological necessity of the first importance, a regulative element in the life of mankind which cannot be dispensed with... But it is not only a biological law but a moral obligation, and, as such, an dispensable factor in civilization.*Germany and the Next War*, (1914)
Friedrich von Bernhardi, German Author (1849-1930)

If you go on with this nuclear arms race, all you are going to do is make the rubble bounce.
Sir Winston Churchill, British Prime Minister(1874-1965)

You cannot prevent and prepare for war at the same time.
Albert Einstein, German-born American
Physicist (1879-1955)

Don't talk to me about naval tradition. It's nothing but rum, sodomy, and the lash.
Sir Winston Churchill, British Prime Minister(1874-1965)

The pioneers of a warless world are the [youth] who refuse military service.
Albert Einstein, German-born American
Physicist (1879-1955)

War is not life: it is a situation, One which may neither be ignored or accepted.
T. S. Eliot, Irish-born American Poet (1888-1965)

We have come to be one of the worst ruled, one of the most completely controlled and dominated Governments in the world — no longer a Government of free opinion, no longer a Government by conviction and vote of the majority, but a Government by the opinion and duress of small groups of dominant men.
Woodrow T. Wilson, American President (1856-1924)

My solution to the problem (of Vietnam) would be to tell them frankly that they've got to draw in their horns and stop their aggression, or we're going to bomb them back into the Stone Age. *Mission with LeMay,* (1965)
Curtis E. LeMay, American General (1906-1990)

Patriots always talk of dying for their country and never of killing for their country.
>     Bertrand Russell, British Philosopher (1872-1970)

Once lead this people into war and they'll forget there ever was such a thing as tolerance. To fight you must be brutal and ruthless and the spirit of ruthlessness will enter into the very fiber of our national life, infecting Congress, the courts,  the policeman on the beat, the man in the street.
>     Woodrow T. Wilson, American President (1856-1924)

In Flanders Fields
In Flanders fields the poppies blow
Between the crosses, row on row,
That mark our place; and in the sky
The larks, still bravely singing, fly
Scarce heard among the guns below.

We are the Dead. Short days ago
We lived, felt dawn, saw sunset glow,
Loved and were loved, and now we lie
In Flanders fields.
Take up our quarrel with the foe:
To you from failing hands we throw
The torch; be yours to hold it high.
If ye break faith with us who die
We shall not sleep, though poppies grow
*In Flanders Fields*, (1917)
>     John McCrae, Canadian Army Doctor (1872-1918)

For a strong adversary (corps) the opposition of twenty-four squadrons and twelve guns ought not to have appeared very serious, but in war the psychological factors are often decisive. An adversary who feels inferior is in reality so.
Carl Gustav Baron Von Mannerheim, Finnish General
(1867-1951)

The most persistent sound which reverberates through man's history is the beating of war drums.
Arthur Koestler, Hungarian-born British Author
(1905-1983)

The quickest way of ending a war is to lose it.
*Second Thoughts on James Burnham*
George Orwell, British Author (1903-1950)

When we, the Workers, all demand:
What are we fighting for?
Then, then we'll end that stupid crime,
that devil's madness — War.
*Michael.*
Robert William Service, Scottish-born Canadian Poet
(1874-1958)

Two armies that fight each other is like one large army that commits suicide. *Le Feu* (1915)
Henri Barbusse, French Author (1873-1935)

The only defence is in offence, which means that you have to kill more women and children more quickly than the enemy if you want to save yourselves.
Stanley Baldwin, British Prime Minister (1867-1947)

War is not an adventure. It is a disease. It is like typhus.
*Flight to Arras,* (1942)
Antoine de Saint-Exupéry, French Author (1900-1944)

East and west on fields forgotten
Bleach the bones of comrades slain,
Lovely lads and dead and rotten;
None that go return again.
*A Shropshire Lad.*
A.E Housman, British Author (1859-1936)

You may not be interested in war, but war is interested
in you.
Leon Trotsky, Russian Politician (1879-1940)

The pallor of girls' brows shall be their pall;
Their flowers the tenderness of patient minds,
And each slow dusk a drawing-down of blinds.
*Anthem for Doomed Youth.* (1914)
Wilfred Owen, British Poet (1893-1918)

I don't know whether war is an interlude during peace,
or peace an interlude during war.
Georges Clemenceau, French Politician (1843-1929)

Red lips are not so red
As the stained stones kissed by the English dead.
*Greater Love,* (1914)
Wilfred Owen, British Poet (1893-1918

You will be home before the leaves have fallen from the
trees.
Said to troops leaving for the front, Aug 1914
Kaiser Wilhelm II, King of Prussia (1859-1941)

I think it is well also for the man in the street to realise that there is no power on earth that can protect him from being bombed. Whatever people may tell him, the bomber will always get through, and it is very easy to understand that, if you realise the area of space.

Stanley Baldwin, British Prime Minister (1867-1947)

If any question why we died, Tell them, because our fathers lied.

Rudyard Kipling, British Author (1865-1936)

Common experience shows how much rarer is moral courage than physical bravery. A thousand men will march to the mouth of the cannon where one man will dare espouse an unpopular cause ... True courage and manhood come from the consciousness of the right attitude toward the world, the faith in one's purpose, and the sufficiency of one's own approval as a justification for one's own acts. *Resist Not Evil.*

Clarence Darrow, American Lawyer (1857-1938)

We have all lost the war. All Europe. *The Ladybird.*

D.H Lawrence, British Author (1885-1930)

This war, like the next war, is a war to end war.

Referring to the opinion that
World War I would be the last major war
David Lloyd George, British Prime Minister (1863-1945)

War is too serious a matter to entrust to military men.

Georges Clemenceau, French Politician (1843-1929)

War? War is an organized bore.
*Yankee from Olympus.*

Oliver Wendell Holmes Jr, American Jurist (1841-1935)

If, therefore, war should ever come between these two countries, which Heaven forbid! it will not, I think, be due to irresistible natural laws, it will be due to the want of human wisdom.
*Referring to the UK and Germany in Nov 1911*
Andrew Bonar Law, Canadian-born
British Prime Minister (1858-1923)

Yes, we have won the war, and not without difficulty. But now we must win the peace, and perhaps that will be harder.
Georges Clemenceau, French Politician (1843-1929)

It is my Royal and Imperial Command that you ... exterminate first the treacherous English, and... walk over General French's contemptible little Army.
*Referring to the British Expeditionary Force; veterans of this force became known as 'Old Contemptibles'*
Kaiser Wilhelm II, King of Prussia (1859-1941

War would end if the dead could return.
Stanley Baldwin, British Prime Minister (1867-1947)

I could not give my name to aid the slaughter in this war, fought on both sides for grossly material ends, which did not justify the sacrifice of a single mother's son. Clearly I must continue to oppose it, and expose it, to all whom I could reach with voice or pen.
*The Home Front,* (1932)
Sylvia Pankhurst, British Suffragette (1882-1960)

When war is declared, truth is the first casualty.
*Falsehood in Wartime,* (1928)
Arthur Ponsonby, British Politician (1871-1946)

A man seeks to control and harmonize his life so that he may be at peace. But nature, perhaps, is not ready to round off so small a piece of creation, and he finds himself swept into conflict by impulses that are part of some large whole. There are greater issues than his comfort.
Charles Horton Cooley, American Author 1864-1929)

Man, it seemed, had been created to jab the life out of Germans. *Memoirs of an Infantry Officer*, (1930)
Siegfried Sassoon, British Poet (1886-1967)

Everything, everything in war is barbaric... But the worst barbarity of war is that it forces men collectively to commit acts against which individually they would revolt with their whole being. *War, Peace and the Future*, (1916)
Ellen Key, Swedish Author (1849-1926)

So long as goverments set the example of killing their enemies, private citizens will occasionally kill theirs.
Elbert Hubbard, American Author (1856-1915)

If I were fierce and bald and short of breath,
I'd live with scarlet Majors at the Base,
And speed glum heroes up the line to death.
*Base Details*, (1918)
Siegfried Sassoon, British Poet (1886-1967)

What a country calls its vital... interests are not things that help its people live, but things that help it make war. Petroleum is a more likely cause of international conflict than wheat.
*Ecrits historiques et politiques*, (1960)
Simone Weil, French Author (1909-1943)

Now all roads lead to France
And heavy is the tread
Of the living; but the dead
Returning lightly dance.
*Roads*
                  Edward Thomas, British Poet (1878-1917)

Can anything be stupider than that a man has the right
to kill me because he lives on the other side of a river
and his ruler has a quarrel with mine, though I have not
quarrelled with him? *Bethink Yourselves.*
                  Leo Tolstoy, Russian Author (1828-1910)

When you march into France, let the last man on the
right brush the Channel with his sleeve.
                  Alfred Graf von Schlieffen, German General
                  (1833-1913)

Probably the Battle of Waterloo was won on the playing-
fields of Eton, but the opening battles of all subsequent
wars have been lost there.
*The Lion and the Unicorn*, (1941)
                  George Orwell, British Author (1903-1950)

It's easy to fight when everything's right
And you're mad with the thrill and the glory;
It's easy to cheer when victory's near,
And wallow in fields that are gory.
It's a different song when everything's wrong,
When you're feeling infernally mortal;
When it's ten against one, and hope there is none,
Buck up, little soldier, and chortle!
*Carry On.*
                  Robert William Service, Scottish-born Canadian Poet
                  (1874-1958)

Airplanes are interesting toys, but of no military value.
Ferdinand Foch, French General (1851-1929)

War brought more glory to their eyes than blood,
And gave their laughs more glee than shakes a child.
Wilfred Owen, British Poet (1893–1918)

Safe with his wound, a citizen of life,
He hobbled blithely through the garden gate,
And thought: 'Thank God they had to amputate!'
*The One-Legged Man.*
Siegfried Sassoon, British Poet (1886-1967

Formerly, a nation that broke the peace did not trouble to try and prove to the world that it was done solely from higher motives... Now war has a bad conscience. Now every nation assures us that it is bleeding for a human cause, the fate of which hangs in the balance of its victory... No nation dares to admit the guilt of blood before the world. *War, Peace and the Future,* (1916)
Ellen Key, Swedish Author (1849-1926)

If I should die, think only this of me:
That there's some corner of a foreign field
That is forever England.
*The Soldier*
Rupert Brooke, British Poet (1887-1915)

I had always to remember that I could have lost the war in an afternoon.
Referring to the Battle of Jutland
Lord John Jellicoe, British Admiral (1859-1935)

It takes 15,000 casualties to train a major general.
Ferdinand Foch, French General (1851-1929)

Tweedledum and Tweedledee
Agreed to have a battle;
For Tweedledum said Tweedledee
Had spoiled his nice new rattle.
*Through the Looking-Glass*, (1872)
Lewis Carroll, British Author (1832-1898)

What they could do with round here is a good war.
*Mother Courage and her Children*, (1941)
Bertold Brecht, German Dramatist. (1898-1956)

I am making this statement as a wilful defiance of military authority because I believe that the War is being deliberately prolonged by those who have the power to end it. *Memoirs of an Infantry Officer*, (1930)
Siegfried Sassoon, British Poet (1886-1967)

Come on, you sons of bitches! Do you want to live for ever?
Remark during resistance at Belleau Wood, June 1918
Dan Daly, American Sgt Major (1873-1937)

If there is ever another war in Europe, it will come out of some damned silly thing in the Balkans.
Remark to Ballen, shortly before his death
Otto von Bismarck, German Statesman (1815-1898)

Is there any man, is there any woman, let me say any child here that does not know that the seed of war in the modern world is industrial and commercial rivalry?
Woodrow T. Wilson, American President (1856-1924)

All wars are planned by old men In council rooms apart.
*Two Sides of War.*
Grantland Rice, American Sportswriter (1880-1954)

61

And the various holds and rolls and throws and breakfalls
Somehow or other I always seemed to put
In the wrong place. And as for war, my wars
Were global from the start.
*A Map of Verona*, (1946)
Henry Reed, British Poet (1914-1986)

Madam, I am the civilization they are fighting to defend.
*Oxford Now and Then.*
Replying to criticism that he was not fighting
to defend civilization, during World War I
William Heathcote Garrod, British Scholar (1878-1960)

'Good morning; good morning!' the general said
When we met him last week on our way to the line.
Now the soldiers he smiled at are most of 'em dead,
And we're cursing his staff for incompetent swine.
*The General*, (1918)
Siegfried Sassoon, British Poet (1886-1967)

Fire — without hatred.
Giving the order to open fire at the siege of the Alcázar
Antonio Rivera, Spanish General (1903-1936)

There is such a thing as a man being too proud to fight.
Address to foreign-born citizens, May 1915
Woodrow T. Wilson, American President (1856-1925)

My centre is giving way, my right is in retreat; situation
excellent. I shall attack.
Ferdinand Foch, French General (1851-1929)

War hath no fury like a non-combatant.
*Disenchantment*, (1922)
C.E Montague, British Author (1867-1928)

I have many times asked myself whether there can be more potent advocates of peace upon earth through the years to come than this massed multitude of silent witnesses to the desolation of war. *Silent Cities,* (1922)
Referring to the many World War I graves in Flanders
George V, British Monarch (1865-1936)

Every position must be held to the last man: there must be no retirement. With our backs to the wall, and believing in the justice of our cause, each one of us must fight on to the end.
Sir Douglas Haig, British General (1861-1928)

War is so unjust and ugly that all who wage it must try to stifle the voice of conscience within themselves.
Leo Tolstoy, Russian Author (1828-1910)

Drake he's in his hammock till the
great Armadas come.
Capten, art tha sleepin' there below?
Slung atween the round shot, listenin' for the drum,
An dreamin' arl the time o' Plymouth Hoe.
*Drake's Drum,* (1896)
Sir Henry John Newbolt, British Poet (1862-1938)

Sometime they'll give a war and nobody will come.
*The People,Yes,* (1940)
Carl Sandburg, American Poet (1878-1967)

Yes; quaint and curious war is! You shoot a fellow down You'd treat if met where any bar is, Or help to half-a-crown.
Thomas Hardy, British Author (1840-1928)

My only fear is that the Zulu will not fight.
Frederick T. Chelmsford, British General (1827-1905)

War is God's way of teaching Americans geography.
Ambrose Bierce, American Author (1842-1914)

I think of this war as it really is, not as the people at home imagine, with a hoorah! and a roar. It is very serious, very grim.
Manfred von Richthofen, German Airman (1892-1918)

I don't mind your being killed, but I object to your being taken prisoner.
To the Prince of Wales during World War I
Horatio Kitchener, British General (1850-1916)

A war of which we could say it left nothing to be desired will probably never exist. *Mother Courage*, (1941)
Bertold Brecht, German Dramatist (1898-1956)

In the fight between you and the world, back the world.
Franz Kafka, Austrian Author (1883-1924)

And when the war is done and youth stone dead
I'd toddle safely home and die — in bed.
*Base Details*, (1918)
Siegfried Sassoon, British Poet (1886-1967)

The war we have just been through, though it was shot through with terror, is not to be compared with the war we would have to face next time. *Mr Wilson's War.*
Woodrow Wilson, American President (1856-1925)

O Lord our God, help us tear their soldiers to bloody shreds with our shells; help us to cover their smiling fields with the pale forms of their patriot dead; help us to drown the thunder of the guns with the shrieks of their wounded, writhing in pain; help us to lay waste

their humble homes with a hurricane of fire; help us to wring the hearts of their unoffending widows with unavailing grief; help us to turn them out roofless with their little children to wander unfriended the wastes of their desolated land in rags and hunger and thirst, sports of the sun flames of summer and the icy winds of winter, broken in spirit, worn with travail, imploring Thee for the refuge of the grave and denied it.
*The War Prayer,* (1905)
> Mark Twain, American Author (1835-1910)

It is easier to lead men to combat, stirring up their passions, than to restrain them and direct them toward the patient labors of peace. *Journals.*
> André Gide, French Author (1869-1951)

What the youthful leader accomplished in aerial combat will never be forgotten by Me, My army and the German people.
> Referring to Baron von Richtofen
> Kaiser Wilhelm II, King of Prussia (1859-1941)

War is so unjust and ugly that all who wage it must try to stifle the voice of conscience within themselves.
> Leo Tolstoy, Russian Author (1828-1910)

The Boers have provided themselves too hard a nut to crack for even Great Britain with all her might. Five years after a devastating war they are again in the ascendancy. They cannot be suppressed! They are bound to become a great nation because they possess the three essential qualities which go to the making of a great nation: 'They are good fathers, good fighters and good Christians'.
> Theodore Roosevelt, American President (1858-1919)

Once lead this people into war and they'll forget there ever was such a thing as tolerance. *Mr Wilson's War.*
Woodrow T. Wilson, American President
(1856-1925)

I bear no hatred against England; I hate no one; everyone is welcome in our country, whether he be a Frenchman, or German, or American or Englishman, I am always ready to hand him the hand of friendship. But let the entire world come and try to tread on me and try to put its foot on my neck, and try to take away the freedom of my country and my nation — then, with a guard of twenty burghers, I shall fight, yes, against the whole world, until I am either free or dead.
Piet Joubert, Boer General (1831-1900)

War on the other hand is such a terrible thing, that no man, especially a Christian man, has the right to assume the responsibility of starting it.
Leo Tolstoy, Russian Author (1828-1910)

We are not interested in the possibilities of defeat; they do not exist.
Queen Victoria, British Monarch (1819-1901)

It is a worthy thing to fight for one's freedom; it is another sight finer to fight for another man's. And I think this is the first time it has been done.
Referring to the Spanish American War in 1899
Mark Twain, American Author (1835-1910)

War knows no power. Safe shall be my going,
Secretly armed against all death's endeavour;
Safe though all safety's lost; safe where men fall;
And if these poor limbs die, safest of all. *Safety.*
Rupert Brooke, British Poet (1887-1915)

War! When I but think of this word, I feel bewildered, as though they were speaking to me of sorcery, of the Inquisition, of a distant, finished, abominable, monstrous, unnatural thing. When they speak to us of cannibals, we smile proudly, as we proclaim our superiority to these savages. Who are the real savages? Those who struggle in order to eat those whom they vanquish, or those who struggle merely to kill?

> Guy de Maupassant, French Author (1850-1893)

The Boers are not like the Sudanese, who stood up to a fair fight.They're always running away on their little ponies.

> Horatio Kitchener, British General (1850-1916)

Oh, if the Queen were a man, she would like to go and give those horrid Russians such a beating.

> Response to war against Turkey in 1877
> Queen Victoria, British Monarch (1819-1901)

The most powerful weapon on earth is the human soul on fire.

> Ferdinand Foch, French General (1851-1929)

They have always taught and trained you to believe it to be your patriotic duty to go to war and to have yourselves slaughtered at their command. But in all the history of the world you, the people, have never had a voice in declaring war, and strange as it certainly appears, no war by any nation in any age has ever been declared by the people.

> Eugene Debs, American Politician (1855-1926)

A war for a great principle ennobles a nation.

> Albert Pike, American Lawyer (1809-1891)

As long as war is regarded as wicked, it will always have its fascination. When it is looked upon as vulgar, it will cease to be popular. *The Critic as Artist*, (1891)
Oscar Wilde, Irish Author (1854-1900)

Every government has as much of a duty to avoid war as a ship's captain has to avoid a shipwreck.
Guy de Maupassant, French Author (1850-1893)

The river of death has brimmed its banks.
And England's far and honour a name.
But the voice of a schoolboy rallies the ranks:
'Play up! play up! and play the game!' *Vitaï Lampada.*
Sir Henry John Newbolt, British Poet (1862-1938)

Insanity in individuals is something rare — but in groups, parties, nations and epochs, it is the rule.
Friedrich Nietzsche, German Philosopher (1844-1900)

Man is the only animal that deals in that atrocity of atrocities, War. He is the only one that gathers his brethren about him and goes forth in cold blood and calm pulse to exterminate his kind. He is the only animal that for sordid wages will march out... and help to slaughter strangers of his own species who have done him no harm and with whom he has no quarrel.... And in the intervals between campaigns he washes the blood off his hands and works for "the universal brotherhood of man" — with his mouth.
Mark Twain, American Author (1835-1910)

We look forward to the time when the Power of Love will replace the Love of Power. Then will our world know the blessings of Peace.
William E. Gladstone, British Prime Minister
(1809-1888)

Teach your children what we have taught our children, that the earth is our mother. Whatever befalls the earth, befalls the children of the earth. If people spit upon the ground, they spit upon themselves. This we know. All things are connected like the blood which unites our family. If we kill the snakes, the field mice will multiply and destroy our corn. All things are connected. Whatever befalls the earth, befalls the children of the earth. Human beings did not weave the web of life: they are merely a strand in it. Whatever they do to the web, they do to themselves. Speech in 1854.

> Seattle, Suquamish Chief (1786-1866)

Yet each man kills the thing he loves, By each let this be heard, Some do it with a bitter look, Some with a flattering word. The coward does it with a kiss, The brave man with a sword!

> Oscar Wilde, Irish Author (1854-1900)

The sand of the desert is sodden red,
Red with the wreck of a square that broke;
The gatling's jammed and the colonel dead,
And the regiment blind with the dust and smoke.

> Sir Henry Newbolt, British Poet (1862-1938)

Don't cheer, boys; the poor devils are dying.

> Restraining his victorious crew during the naval battle
> off Santiago in the Spanish-American War
> John Woodward Philip, American Naval Officer
> (1840-1900)

The stench of the trail of Ego in our History. It is ego - ego, the fountain cry, origin, sole source of war.
*Beauchamp's Career.*

> George Meredith, British Author (1828-1909)

Let's kick their ass and get the hell out of here.
George Armstrong Custer, American General
(1839-1876)

Law never made men a whit more just; and by means of their respect for it, even the well-disposed are daily made the agents of injustice. A common and natural result of an undue respect for law is that you may see a file of soldiers, colonel, captain, corporal, privates, powder-monkeys, and all marching in admirable order over hill and dale to the wars, against their wills, ay, against their common sense and consciences, which makes it very steep marching indeed, and produces a palpitation of the heart. They have no doubt that it is a damnable business in which they are concerned; they are all peaceably inclined. Now, what are they? Men at all? or small movable forts and magazines, at the service of some unscrupulous man in power? The mass of men serve the State thus, not as men mainly, but as machines, with their bodies.... In most cases there is no free exercise whatever of the judgment or of the moral sense; but they put themselves on a level with wood and earth and stones; and wooden men can perhaps be manufactured that will serve the purpose as well.
*On the Duty of Civil Disobedience* Pt.1, (1849)
Henry David Thoreau, American Author (1817-1862)

I got there fustest with the mostest.
Nathan Bedford Forrest, American General (1821-1877)

If men make war in slavish obedience to rules, they will fail.
Ulysses S. Grant, American General (1822-1885)

There is many a boy here today who looks on war as all glory, but, boys, it is all hell. You can bear this warning voice to generations yet to come. I look upon war with horror.

William Tecumseh Sherman, American General
(1820-1891)

General. Soldiering has one great trap. To be a good soldier you must love the army. To be a good commander you must be willing to order the death of the thing you love. We do not fear our own death, you and I. But there comes a time... we are never quite prepared for so many to die. Oh, we do expect the occasional empty chair, a salute to fallen comrades. But this war goeson and on, and the men die, and the price gets ever higher. We are prepared to lose some of us, but we are never prepared to lose all of us. And there is the great trap, General. When you attack you must hold nothing back, you must commit yourself totally. We are adrift here in a sea of blood and I want it to end. I want this to be the final battle.

To General James Longstreet at Gettysburg, 1863
Robert E. Lee, American General (1807-1880)

I can make men follow me to hell.

Philip Kearny, American General (1815-1862)

Military glory — the attractive rainbow that rises in showers of blood.

Abraham Lincoln, American President (1809-1865)

Experience proves that the man who obstructs a war in which his nation is engaged, no matter whether right or wrong, occupied no enviable place in life or history. Better for him, individually, to advocate 'war, pestilence, and famine,' than to act as obstructionist to a war already begun.

Ulysses S. Grant, American General (1822-1885)

Come on boys! Give them the cold steel! Who will follow me?

At Gettysburg where he died
Lewis Armistead, American General (1817-1863)

The brave men, living and dead, who struggled here, have consecrated it, above our poor power to add or detract. The world will little note, nor long remember, what we say here, but it can never forget what they did here.

Address at Gettysburg, 1863
Abraham Lincoln, American President (1809-1865)

The only good Indian is a dead Indian.

Philip Henry Sheridan, American General (1831-1888)

It is only those who have neither fired a shot nor heard the shrieks and groans of the wounded who cry aloud for blood, more vengeance, more desolation. War is hell.

William Tecumseh Sherman, American General
(1820-1891)

It is well that war is so terrible — we should grow too fond of it.

At the battle of Fredericksburg,1862
Robert E. Lee, American General (1807-1880)

72

No terms except unconditional and immediate surrender can be accepted. I propose to move immediately upon your works.

> During siege of Fort Donelson in 1862
> Ulysses S. Grant, American General (1822-1885)

What a cruel thing is war: to separate and destroy families and friends, and mar the purest joys and happiness God has granted us in this world; to fill our hearts with hatred instead of love for our neighbors, and to devastate the fair face of this beautiful world.

> Letter to his wife
> Robert E. Lee, American General (1807-1880)

I leaned down from the saddle, rammed the muzzle of the carbine into the stomach of my man and pulled the trigger. He tried to get his bayonet up to meet me; but he was too slow, for the carbine blew a hole as big as my arm clear through him.

> At the first Bull Run
> William W. Blackford, Virginian Cavalry Officer

Give me the money that has been spent in war and I will clothe every man, woman, and child in an attire of which kings and queens will be proud. I will build a schoolhouse in every valley over the whole earth. I will crown every hillside with a place of worship consecrated to peace.

> Charles Sumner, American Polititcian (1811-1874)

I am tired and sick of war, its glory is all, moonshine ... war is hell.

> William Tecumseh Sherman, American General
> (1820-1891)

I never advocated war except as a means of peace.
Ulysses S. Grant, American General (1822-1885)

We saw the lightning and that was the guns and then we heard the thunder and that was the big guns; and then we heard the rain falling and that was the blood falling; and when we came to get in the crops, it was dead men that we reaped.
Harriet Tubman, American Civil Rights Activist (1820-1913)

At what point shall we expect the approach of danger? By what means shall we fortify against it? Shall we expect some transatlantic military giant to step the ocean and crush us at a blow? Never! All the armies of Europe, Asia, and Africa combined, with all the treasure of the earth in their military chests; with a Buonaparte for a commander, could not by force take a drink from the Ohio, or make a track on the Blue Ridge, in the trial of a thousand years.At what point then is the approach of danger to be expected? I answer, if it ever reach us, it must spring up amongst us. It cannot come from abroad. If destruction be our lot, we ourselves must be its author and finisher. As a nation of freemen, we must live through all time, or die by suicide.
Abraham Lincoln, American President (1809-1865)

...but one of them would make war rather than let the nation survive, and the other would accept war rather than let it perish, and the war came.
Abraham Lincoln, American President (1809-1865)

I can stand out the war with any man.
Florence Nightingale, British Nurse (1820-1910)

They dashed on towards that thin red line tipped with steel.
> Russian charge against the British at Balaclava in 1854
> William Howard Russell, British Author (1820-1907)

C'est magnifique, mais ce n'est pas la guerre.
It is magnificent, but it is not war.
> Referring to the disastrous Charge of the
> Light Brigade at the Battle of Balaclava, Oct 1854
> Pierre Bosquet, French Field Marshall (1810-1861)

Till the war-drum throbbed no longer,
and the battle-flags were furl'd
In the Parliament of man,
the Federation of the world.
*Locksley Hall,* (1842)
> Alfred Lord Tennyson, British Poet (1809-1892)

War is a quarrel between two thieves too cowardly to fight their own battle; therefore they take boys from one village and another village, stick them into uniforms, equip them with guns, and let them loose like wild beasts against each other.
> Thomas Carlyle, British Author (1795-1881)

The Angel of Death has been abroad throughout the land: you may almost hear the beating of his wings.
> Referring to the Crimean War, Feb 1855
> John Bright, British Politician (1811-1889)

I stand at the altar of the murdered men, and, while I live, I fight their cause.
> Florence Nightingale, British Nurse (1820-1910)

War is an ugly thing, but not the ugliest of things. The decayed and degraded state of moral and patriotic feeling which thinks that nothing is worth war is much worse. The person who has nothing for which he is willing to fight, nothing which is more important than his own personal safety, is a miserable creature, and has no chance of being free unless made or kept so by the exertions of better men than himself.
John Stuart Mill, British Philosopher (1806-1873)

War is the continuation of politics by other means.
*Vom Kriege*, (1832)
Carl von Clausewitz, Prussian General (1780-1831)

There rises the sun of Austerlitz.
Said at the Battle of Austerlitz Dec,1805 at Napoleon's victory over the Russians and Austrians
Napoleon Bonaparte, French Emperor (1769-1821)

I don't care for war, there's far too much luck in it for my liking.
Said after the narrow bloody French victory at Solferino June, 1859
Charles Louis Napoleon III, French Emperor (1808-1876)

The whole art of war consists in getting at what is on the other side of the hill.
Arthur Wellesley (Duke of Wellington), British General (1769-1852)

Never interrupt your enemy when he is making a mistake.
Napoleon Bonaparte, French Emperor (1769-1821)

Read over and over again the campaigns of Alexander, Hannibal, Caesar, Gustavus, Turenne, Eugene and Frederic... This is the only way to become a great general and master the secrets of the art of war.
Napoleon Bonaparte, French Emperor (1769-1821)

Up, Guards, and at 'em.
Order given at the Battle of Waterloo, June 1815
Arthur Wellesley (Duke of Wellington), British General
(1769-1852)

It has been a damned serious business — Blücher and I have lost 30,000 men. It has been a damned nice thing — the nearest run thing you ever saw in your life... By God! I don't think it would have done if I had not been there.
Referring to the Battle of Waterloo
Arthur Wellesley (Duke of Wellington) British General
(1769-1852)

Yes, and they went down very well too.
Referring to the French cavalry at the Battle of Waterloo
Arthur Wellesley (Duke of Wellington) British General
(1769-1852)

When can their glory fade?
O the wild charge they made!
All the world wonder'd.
Honor the charge they made!
Honor the Light Brigade,
Noble six hundred!"
*The Charge of the Light Brigade*
Alfred Lord Tennyson, English Poet (1809-1892)

Nothing except a battle lost can be half as melancholy as a battle won.
> Arthur Wellesley (Duke of Wellington), British General
> (1769-1852)

All those who seek to destroy the liberties of a democratic nation ought to know that war is the surest and shortest means to accomplish it.
> Alexis de Tocqueville, French Historian (1805-1859)

A battle of giants.
> Said to Samuel Rogers at the Battle of Waterloo
> Arthur Wellesley (Duke of Wellington), British General
> (1769-1852)

War, war is still the cry, 'War even to the knife!'
*Childe Harold's Pilgrimage*, (1812)
> George Gordon Noel Byron, British Poet (1788-1824)

Take my word for it, if you had seen but one day of war, you would pray to Almighty God that you might never see such a thing again.
> Arthur Wellesley (Duke of Wellington), British General
> (1769-1852)

It's the most beautiful battlefield I've ever seen.
> Referring to the destruction at the
> Borodino, near Moscow, after the battle Sept, 1812
> Napoleon Bonaparte, French Emperor (1769-1821)

As Lord Chesterfield said of the generals of his day, 'I only hope that when the enemy reads the list of their names, he trembles as I do.
> Arthur Wellesley (Duke of Wellington), British General
> (1769-1852)

There are only two forces in the world, the sword and the spirit. In the long run the sword will always be conquered by the spirit.

Napoleon Bonaparte, French Emperor (1769-1821)

In war more than anywhere else in the world things happen differently from what we had expected, and look differently when near from what they did at a distance. *On War.*

Carl von Clausewitz, Prussian General (1780-1871)

War ... should only be declared by the authority of the people, whose toils and treasures are to support its burdens, instead of the government which is to reap its fruits. *Universal Peace.*

James Madison, American President (1751–1836)

Rascals, would you live for ever?

Addressed to reluctant soldiers
at the Battle of Kolin, June 1757
Frederick the Great, King of Prussia (1712-1786)

Stand your ground. Don't fire unless fired upon, but if they mean to have a war, let it begin here!

Command given at the start of the Battle of Lexington.
John Parker, American General (1729-1775)

Soldiers win battles and generals get the credit.

Napoleon Bonaparte, French Emperor (1769-1821)

Everything in war is simple, but the simplest thing is difficult. The difficulties accumulate and end by producing a kind of friction that is inconceivable unless one has experienced war.

Carl von Clausewitz, Prussian General (1780-1871)

Now, gentlemen, let us do something today which the world may talk of hereafter.
> To Horatio Nelson at the Battle of Trafalgar in 1805
> Cuthbert Collingwood, British Admiral (1748-1810)

You must consider every man your enemy who speaks ill of your king; and ... you must hate a Frenchman as you hate the devil. *Life of Nelson.*
> Horatio Nelson, British Naval Lord (1758-1805)

Yonder are the Hessians. They were bought for seven pounds and tenpence a man. Are you worth more? Prove it. Tonight the American flag floats from yonder hill or Molly Stark sleeps a widow!
> Said at the Battle of Bennington in 1777
> John Stark, American General (1728-1822)

Man is the only animal who causes pain to others with no other object than wanting to do so.
> Arthur Schopenhauer, German Philosopher (1788-1860)

War is thus divine in itself, since it is a law of the world. War is divine through its consequences of a supernatural nature which are as much general as particular... War is divine in the mysterious glory that surrounds it and in the no less inexplicable attraction that draws us to it.... War is divine by the manner in which it breaks out.
> Joseph De Maistre, French Diplomat (1753–1821)

No power but Congress can declare war, but what is the value of this constitutional provision, if the President of his own authority may make such military movements as must bring on war?
> Daniel Webster, American Politician (1782-1852)

The quarrels of popes and kings, with wars and pestilences in every page; the men all so good for nothing, and hardly any women at all — it is very tiresome.
Jane Austen, British Author (1775-1817)

An honorable Peace is and always was my first wish! I can take no delight in the effusion of human Blood; but, if this War should continue, I wish to have the most active part in it.
John Paul Jones, Scottish-born American Admiral (1747-1792)

Turkey is a dying man. We may endeavor to keep him alive, but we shall not succeed. He will, he must die.
Emperor Nicholas I, Russia Monarch (1796-1855)

War is the domain of physical exertion and suffering.
Carl von Clausewitz, Prussian General (1780-1871)

Don't fire until you see the whites of their eyes.
Command given at the Battle of Bunker Hill, 1775
William Prescott, American General (1726-1795)

Every citizen should be a soldier. This was the case with the Greeks and Romans, and must be that of every free state.
Thomas Jefferson, American President (1743-1826)

The bad thing of war is, that it makes more evil people than it can take away.
Emmanuel Kant, German Philosopher (1724-1804)

Elevate them guns a little lower.
Order to the artillery at the Battle of New Orleans
Andrew Jackson, American General (1767-1845)

Scots, wha hae wi' Wallace bled,
Scots, wham Bruce has aften led,
Welcome to your gory bed,
Or to victorie.
*Scots, Wha Hae*
Robert Burns, Scottish Poet (1759-1796)

No one starts a war — or rather no one in his senses ought to do so — without first being clear in his mind what he intends to achieve in that war and how he intends to conduct it.
Carl von Clausewitz, Prussian General (1780-1831)

War — An act of violence whose object is to constrain the enemy, to accomplish our will.
George Washington, American President (1732-1799)

War seems to be one of the most salutary phenomena for the culture of human nature; and it is not without regret that I see it disappearing more and more from the scene.
Karl Wilhelm von Humboldt, German Politcian
(1767-1835)

The Minstrel Boy to the war has gone,
In the ranks of death you'll find him;
His father's sword he has girded on,
And his wild harp slung behind him.
*Irish Melodies*, '*The Minstrel Boy*', (1807)
Thomas Moore, Irish Poet (1779-1852)

I heard the bullets whistle, and believe me, there is something charming in the sound.
Referring to a skirmish in the French and Indian War
George Washington, American President (1732-1799)

Civil war? What does that mean? Is there any foreign war? Isn't every war fought between men, between brothers?

Victor Hugo, French Author (1802-1885)

Gentlemen of the French Guard, fire first!

Said at the Battle of Fontenoy in 1745
Charles Hay, British General (1740-1811)

Be at war with your vices, at peace with your neighbors, and let every new year find you a better man.

Benjamin Franklin, American Statesman (1706-1790)

War is an instrument entirely inefficient toward redressing wrong; and multiplies, instead of indemnifying losses.

Thomas Jefferson, American President (1743-1826)

To each of my Nephews, William Augustine Washington, George Lewis, George Steptoe Washington, Bushrod Washington, and Samuel Washington, I give one of my swords or Cutteaux of which I may be Possesed; and they are to chose in the order they are named. These Swords are accompanied with an injuction not to unsheath them for the purpose of shedding blood, except it be for self defense, or in the defense of their Country and its rights; and in the latter case, to keep them unsheathed, and prefer falling with them in their hands, to the relenquishment thereof.

From the last will and testament
George Washington, American President (1732-1799)

We must all hang together, or most assuredly we shall all hang separately.

At the signing of *The Declaration of Independence*
Benjamin Franklin, American Statesman (1706-1790)

War involves in its progress such a train of unforeseen and unsupposed circumstances that no human wisdom can calculate the end. It has but one thing certain, and that is to increase taxes.
>Thomas Paine, British Author (1737-1809)

All wars are civil wars, because all men are brothers.
>François Fenelon, French Bishop (1651-1715)

Man has no right to kill his brother. It is no excuse that he does so in uniform: he only adds the infamy of servitude to the crime of murder.
*A Declaration of Rights.*
>Percy Bysshe Shelley, British Poet (1792–1822)

War is the national industry of Prussia.
>Honore Gabriel Riqueti Comte de Mirabeau
>French Statesman (1749-1791)

An empire founded by war has to maintain itself by war.
>Charles de Secondat Baron de Montesquieu
>French Author (1689-1755)

War is the trade of Kings.
>John Dryden, British Poet (1631–1700)

It is forbidden to kill; therefore all murderers are punished unless they kill in large numbers and to the sound of trumpets. *War*
>Voltaire (Francois Marie Arouet), French Philosopher
>(1694-1778)

They now ring the bells, but they will soon wring their hands.
>Response to war with Spain
>Robert Walpole, British Prime Minister (1676-1745)

Most sorts of diversion in men, children, and other animals, are an imitation of fighting.
*Thoughts on Various Subjects*, (1711)
Jonathan Swift, Irish Author (1667-1745)

When civil fury first grew high, And men fell out they knew not why. *Hudibras.*
Samuel Butler, English Author (1612-1680)

How vast those Orbs must be, and how inconsiderable this Earth, the Theatre upon which all our mighty Designs, all our Navigations, and all our Wars are transacted, is when compared to them. A very fit consideration, and matter of Reflection, for those Kings and Princes who sacrifice the Lives of so many People, only to flatter their Ambition in being Masters of some pitiful corner of this small Spot.
Christiaan Huygens, Dutch Scientist (1629–1695)

This is a righteous judgement of god upon these barbarous wretches, who have imbrued their hands in so much innocent blood....
Referring to the storming of Drogheda in Ireland 1649.
Oliver Cromwell, British Lord Protector (1599–1658)

Students of the Ichi school *Way of Strategy* should train from the start with the sword and long sword in either hand. This is a truth: when you sacrifice your life, you must make fullest use of your weaponry. It is false not to do so, and to die with a weapon yet undrawn.
*A Book of Five Rings.*
Miyamoto Musashi, Japanese Samurai (1584-1645)

War makes thieves and peace hangs them.
George Herbert, British Poet (1593-1633)

Once more unto the breach, dear friends, once more, Or close the wall up with our English dead! In peace there's nothing so becomes a man As modest stillness and humility; But when the blast of war blows in our ears, Then imitate the action of the tiger: Stiffen the sinews, summon up the blood.
*King Henry V,* III: 1, (1598)
William Shakespeare, British Playwright (1564-1623)

Cry 'Havoc!' and let slip the dogs of war.
*Julius Caesar,* III:1, (1600)
William Shakespeare, British Playwright (1564-1616)

Farewell the neighing steed and the shrill trump,
The spirit-stirring drum, th'ear piercing fife,
The royal banner, and all quality,
Pride, pomp, and circumstance, of glorious war!
*Othello,* III:3, (1605)
William Shakespeare, British Playwright (1564-1616)

The pen is mightier than the sword.
William Shakespeare, British Playwright (1564-1616)

A just fear of an imminent danger, though there be no blow given, is a lawful cause of war.
Sir Francis Bacon, British Philosopher (1561-1626)

There is plenty of time to win this game, and to thrash the Spaniards too.
Referring to the Armada during a game of bowls, 1588
Sir Francis Drake, British Naval Officer (1540-1596)

I have singed the Spanish king's beard.
Referring to the raid on Cadiz harbour, 1587
Sir Francis Drake, British Naval Officer (1540-1596)

To kill a man is not to defend a doctrine, but to kill a man.
Michael Servetus, Spanish Scholar (1509-1553)

Monarchs ought to put to death the authors and instigators of war, as their sworn enemies and as dangers to their states.
Elizabeth I, British Monarch (1533-1603)

Blood alone moves the wheels of history.
Martin Luther, German Religious Leader (1483-1546)

War is the greatest plague that can afflict humanity, it destroys religion, it destroys states, it destroys families. Any scourge is preferable to it.
Martin Luther, German Religious Leader (1483-1546)

There is no avoiding war; it can only be postponed to the advantage of others.
Niccolo Machiavelli, Italian Statesman (1469-1527)

War should be the only study of a prince. He should consider peace only as a breathing-time, which gives him leisure to contrive, and furnishes as ability to execute, military plans.
Niccolo Machiavelli, Italian Statesman (1469-1527)

War is delightful to those who have not experienced it.
Desiderius Erasmus, German Humanist (1466-1536)

Whoever conquers a free town and does not demolish it commits a great error and may expect to be ruined himself.
Niccolo Machiavelli, Italian Statesman (1469-1527)

In order for a war to be just, three things are necessary. First, the authority of the sovereign.... Secondly, a just cause.... Thirdly ... a rightful intention.
Thomas Aquinas, Italian Saint (1225-1274)

All who surrender will be spared;whoever does not surrender but opposes with struggle and dissension, shall be annihilated.
Genghis Khan, Mongol War Leader (1162-1227)

Those who do not go to war roar like lions.
Kurdish Proverb

The greatest happiness is to vanquish your enemies,to chase them before you, to rob them of their wealth,to see those dear to them bathed in tears, to clasp to your bosom their wives and daughters.
Genghis Khan, Mongol War Leader (1162-1227)

With Heaven's aid I have conquered for you a huge empire. But my life was too short to achieve the conquest of the world. That is left for you.
To his sons at the end of his life<br>Genghis Khan, Mongol War Leader (1162-1227)

The purpose of all war is ultimately peace.
St. Augustine (c.354-430AD)

We British are used to women commanders in war. I am descended from mighty men! But I am not fighting for my kingdom and wealth now. I am fighting as an ordinary person for my lost freedom, my bruised body, and my outraged daughters ...Consider how many of you are fighting — and why! Then you will win this battle, or or perish. That is what I, a woman, plan to do!—let the men live in slavery if they will. *Annals.*

Quotinf Bodecia, Queen of the Icena (Britons)
Gaius Cornelius Tacitus, Roman Historian (c.56-120 AD)

I tell you, my friends, do not be afraid of those who kill the body and after that can do no more. But I will show you whom you should fear: Fear him who, after the killing of the body, has power to throw you into hell. Yes, I tell you, fear him.
Jesus Christ
(c.4 BC-30 AD)

Put up again thy sword into its place: for all they that take the sword shall perish by the sword.

Bible: Matthew 26

If you weigh well the strengths of our armies you will see that in this battle we must conquer or die. This is a woman's resolve. As for the men, they may live or be slaves.

Bodecia, Queen of Icena (Britons) (c.80-30 BC)

... But an hour is coming when everyone who kills you will think that he is offering service to God.

Bible: John 16:2

I came. I saw. I conquered. *Veni, Vidi, Vici.*

Julius Caesar, Roman Emperor (c.100-44 BC)

89

A handful of men, inured to war, proceed to certain victory, while on the contrary, numerous armies of raw and undisciplined troops are but multitudes of men dragged to the slaughter.

Vegetius Flavius Renatus,
Roman Historian (c.301-375 AD)

Beware the leader who bangs the drum of war in order to whip the citizenry into a patriotic fervor. For patriotism is indeed a double- edged sword. It both emboldens the blood, just as it narrows the mind. And when the drums of war have reached a fever pitch and the blood boils with hate and the mind has closed, the leader will have no need in seizing the rights of the citizenry. Rather, the citizenry, infused with fear and patriotism, will offer up all of their rights to the leader and gladly so. How do I know? For this is what I have done. And I am Julius Caesar.

Julius Caesar, Roman Emperor (c.100-44 BC)

Let him who desires peace prepare for war.

Vegetius Flavius Renatus,
Roman Historian (c.301-375 AD)

The Ruler:Therefore the sage, in the exercise of his government,empties their minds, fills their bellies, weakens their wills,and strengthens their bones. He constantly (tries to) keep them without knowledge and without desire, and where there are those who have knowledge, to keep them from presuming to act (on it). When there is this abstinence from action, good order is universal.

Book of Taoism

War is a matter not so much of arms as of expenditure, through which arms may be made of service. *Historia.*

Thucydides, Greek Author (c.460-400 BC)

Fighting for peace is like
screwing for virginity.

Where they make a desert, they call it peace.
Gaius Cornelius Tacitus, Roman Historian (c.56-120 AD)

We find that the Romans owed the conquest of the world to no other cause than continual military training, exact observance of discipline in their camps, and unwearied cultivation of the other arts of war.
Vegetius Flavius Renatus, Roman Historian
(c.301-370 AD)

So, as you go into battle, remember your ancestors and remember your descendants.
Gaius Cornelius Tacitus, Roman Historian(c.56-120 AD)

We are mad, not only individually, but nationally. We check manslaughter and isolated murders; but what of war and the much vaunted crime of slaughtering whole peoples?
Lucius Annaeus Seneca, Spanish-born
Roman Playwright (c.4 BC-65 AD)

When the swords flash let no idea of love, piety, or even the face of your fathers move you.
Julius Caesar, Roman Emperor (c.100-44 BC)

It is sweet and honorable to die for one's country.
Horace Flaccus, Roman Poet (c.65-8 BC)

And when all the world is overcharged with inhabitants, then the last remedy is Warre; which provideth for every man, by Victory, or Death.
Horace Flaccus, Roman Poet (c.65-8 BC)

I prefer the most unfair peace to the most righteous war.
Marcus Tullius Cicero, Roman Statesman (c106-43 BC)

A bad peace is even worse than war.
> Cornelius Tacitus, Roman Historian (c.56-120 AD)

In love there are two evils: war and peace.
> Horace Flaccus, Roman Poet (c.65-8 BC)

The best way of avenging thyself is not to become like the wrong-doer.
> Marcus Aurelius Antoninus, Roman Emperor
> (c.180-121 BC)

Carthage must be destroyed. *Life of Cato.*
> Cato the Elder (Marcius Porcius) Roman Statesman
> (c.234-149 BC)

We will either find a way or make one.
> Hannibal Barca, North African War Lord (c.247-182 BC)

Another such victory and we are undone.
> Pyrrhus Molossian, King of Epirus, (c.318-272 BC)

We make war that we may live in peace.
> Aristotle, Greek Philosopher (c.384-322 BC)

Only the dead have seen the end of war
> Plato, Greek Philospher (c.428-348 BC)

Zeus most glorious and most great, Thundercloud, throned in the heavens! Let not the sun go down and the darkness come, until I cast down headlong the citadel of Priam in flames, and burn his gates with blazing fire, and tear to rags the shirt upon Hector's breast! May many of his men fall about him prone in the dust and bite the earth! *The Iliad.*
> Homer, Greek Poet (c.700 BC

War loves to seek its victims in the young.
Sophocles, Greek Philospher (c.496-406 BC)

The shaft of the arrow had been feathered with one of the eagle's own plumes. We often give our enemies the means of our own destruction.
Aesop, Greek Author (c.600-520 BC)

War never takes a wicked man by chance, the good man always. *Philoctetes,*
Sophocles, Greek Philosopher (c.495–406 BC.)

Know thy lot, Know thine enemies, Know thyself. Know thy enemy and know thy self and you will win a hundred battles.
Sun Tzu Wu, Chinese War Lord (c.500 BC)

Whoever advises a ruler according to Tao opposes conquest by war. Policies of war tend to rebound.
Tao Te Ching (The Way and It's Power) (c.500 BC)

The slaying of multitudes should be mourned with sorrow. A victory should be celebrated with the funeral rite.
Lao-Tzu, Chinese Taoist Philosopher (c.604-531 BC)

In all history, there is no instance of a country having benefited from prolonged warfare. Only one who knows the disastrous effects of a long war can realize the supreme importance of rapidity in bringing it to a close.
Sun Tzu Wu, Chinese War Lord (c.500 BC)

Thus we may know that there are five essentials for victory: (1) He will win who knows when to fight and when not to fight. (2) He will win who knows how to handle both superior and inferior forces. (3) He will win whose army is animated by the same spirit throughout all the ranks. (4) He will win who, prepared himself, waits to take the enemy unprepared. (5) He will win who has military capacity and is not interfered with by his sovereign. Victory lies in the knowledge of these five points. *Art of War.*

Sun Tzu Wu, Chinese War Lord (c.500 BC)

...Scatter thou the people that delight in war.

Bible: Psalms 68:30

Laws are silent in time of war from within. Do not seek it without.

Buddha, Indian Religious Leader (c.563-483 BC)

The sun shall be turned into darkness, and the moon into blood....With Justice he judges and makes war ... He is dressed in a robe dipped in blood and his name is the word of God ... Out of his mouth comes a sharp sword with which to strike down nations. .so you may eat the flesh of kings, generals, and mighty men, of horses and their riders, and the flesh of all people, free and slave, small and great The Messiah slays the Anti Christ and "creates a new heaven and a new earth" and He judges the dead, saves the Christians, and casts the rest into eternal perdition.

Acts of the Apostles

Proclaim this among the nations: Prepare war ... Beat your plowshares into swords, and your pruning hooks into spears; let the weak say, 'I am a warrior.'"

Bible: Joel 3:9,10 (Revised Standard)

Every purpose is established by counsel: and with good advice make war.

Bible: Proverbs 20: 18

But the word of the Lord came to me, saying, Thou hast shed blood abundantly, and hast made great wars: thou shalt not build an house unto my name, because thou hast shed much blood upon the earth in my sight.

Bible: I Chronicles 22:8

Wherefore should the heathen say, Where is their God? let him be known among the heathen in our sight by the revenging of the blood of thy servants which is shed. Revenge for shed blood

Bible: Psalms 79:10

For by wise counsel thou shalt make thy war: and in multitude of counsellors there is safety.

Bible: Proverbs 24:6

So Asa went out against him, and they set the troops in battle array in the Valley of Zephathah at Mareshah. And Asa cried out to the Lord his God, and said, 'Lord, it is nothing for You to help, whether with many or with those who have no power; help us, O Lord our God, for we rest on You, and in Your name we go against this multitude. O Lord, You are our God; do not let man prevail against You!' So the Lord struck the Ethiopians before Asa and Judah, and the Ethiopians fled.

Bible: 2 Chronicles 14:10-12

Well, if you knows of a better 'ole, go to it.
*Fragments from France,* (1917)
    Bruce Bairnsfather, British Cartoonist (1888-1959)

# Peace

I die with the conviction, held since 1968 and Catonsville, that nuclear weapons are the scourge of the earth; to mine for them, manufacture them, deploy them, use them, is a curse against God, the human family, and the earth itself. We have already exploded such weapons in Japan in 1945 and the equivalent of them in Iraq in 1991, in Yugoslavia in 1999, and in Afghanistan in 2001. We left a legacy for other people of deadly radioactive isotopes — a prime counterinsurgency measure. For example, the people of Iraq, Yugoslavia, Afghanistan and Pakistan will be battling cancer, mostly from depleted uranium, for decades. In addition, our nuclear adventurism over 57 years has saturated the planet with nuclear garbage from testing, from explosions in high altitudes (four of these), from 103 nuclear power plants, from nuclear weapons factories that can't be cleaned up — and so on.

Transcribed by his wife Liz McAlister at his death.
Philip Berrigan, American Peace Activist (1923-2002)

In the name of peace
They waged the wars
Ain't they got no shame

Nikki Giovanni, American Poet (b.1943)

97

No matter how big a nation is, it is no stronger that its weakest people, and as long as you keep a person down, some part of you has to be down there to hold him down, so it means you cannot soar as you might otherwise.
Marian Anderson, American Opera Singer (1897-1993)

Fighting for peace is like screwing for virginity.
Author Unknown

The folks who conducted to act on our country on September 11th made a big mistake. They underestimated America. They underestimated our resolve, our determination, our love for freedom.They underestimated the fact that we love a neighbor in need. They underestimated the compassion of our country. I think they underestimated the will and determination of the Commander-in-Chief, too.
George W. Bush, American President (b.1946)

Peace begins with a smile.
Mother Teresa, Macedonian Nun (1910-1997)

To keep 3.5 million people under occupation is bad for us and them.
Sharon's response to Likud concerning the peace talks.
Ariel Sharon, Israeli Prime Minister (b.1928)

I have been true to the principles of nonviolence, developing a stronger and stronger aversion to the ideologies of both the far right and the far left and a deeper sense of rage and sorrow over the suffering they continue to produce all over the world.
Joan Baez, American Folk Singer (b.1941)

Stability and peace in our land will not come from the barrel of a gun, because peace without justice is an impossibility.

Desmond Tutu, South African Bishop (b.1931)

The illiterate of the 21st century will not be those who cannot read and write, but those who cannot learn, unlearn, and relearn.

Alvin Toffler, American Author (b.1928)

All the world over so easy to see, people everywhere just wanna be free. *People Got To Be Free.*

The Rascals, American Rock Band

And ye shall hear of wars and rumours of wars: see that ye be not troubled: for all these things must come to pass, but the end is not yet. For nation shall rise against nation, and kingdom against kingdom: and there shall be famines, and pestilences, and earthquakes, in divers places. All these are the beginning of sorrows.

Bible: Matthew 24:6-8

There is no question but that when one is engaged militarily that there are going to be unintended loss of life.

Donald Rumsfeld, American Defense Secretary (b.1932)

It would be some time before I fully realized that the United States sees little need for diplomacy. Power is enough. Only the weak rely on diplomacy... The Roman Empire had no need for diplomacy. Nor does the United States.

Boutros Boutros-Ghali, Egyptian
Secretary General of the UN (b.1922)

If you are neutral in situations of injustice, you have chosen the side of the oppressor. If an elephant has its foot on the tail of a mouse and you say that you are neutral, the mouse will not appreciate your neutrality.
Desmond Tutu, South African Bishop (b.1931)

It did not take atomic weapons to make man want peace, a peace that would last. But the atomic bomb was the turn of the screw. It has made the prospect of future war unendurable.
Robert Oppenheimer, American Physicist (1904-1967)

Peace, in the sense of absence of war, is of little value to someone who is dying of hunger or cold. Peace can only last where human rights are respected, where people are fed, and where individuals and nations are free.
Dalai Lama, Tibetan (Tenzin Gyatso) (b.1935)

And the evil is done in hopes that evil surrenders, but the deeds of the devil are burned too deep in the embers, and a world of hunger in vengeance will always remember. So please be reassured, we seek no wider war. *We Seek No Wider War,* (1965)
Phil Ochs, American Singer-songwriter (1940-1976)

You know what the trouble with Peace is? No organization. *Mother Courage and her Children,* (1941)
Bertold Brecht, German Dramatist. (1898-1956)

We concluded that tomorrow is a moment of truth for the world. Many nations have voiced a commitment to peace and security, and now they must demonstrate that commitment to peace and security in the only effective way: by supporting the immediate and unconditional disarmament of Saddam Hussein.
George W. Bush, American President (b.1946)

Sometime in your life, hope that you might see one starved man, the look on his face when the bread finally arrives. Hope that you might have baked it or bought or even kneaded it yourself. For that look on his face, for you're meeting his eyes across a piece of bread, you might be willing to lose a lot, or suffer a lot, or die a little, even.

Daniel Berrigan, Jesuit Priest (b.1921)

The fact is that we prepare for war like giants, and for peace like pygmies.

Lester B. Pearson Canadian Prime Minister (1897-1972)

Activism pays the rent on being alive and being here on the planet.

Alice Walker, American Author (b.1944)

You can't separate peace from freedom because no one can be at peace unless he has his freedom.

Malcolm X, American Muslim Leader (1925-1965)

Dear God, Please send to me the spirit of Your peace. Then send, dear Lord, the spirit of peace from me to all the world. Amen.

Marianne Williamson, American Author (b.1952)

The human race has today the means for annihilating itself — either in a fit of complete lunacy, i.e. in a big war... or by the careless handling of atomic technology, through a slow process of poisoning and of deterioration in its genetic structure.

Max Born, German Scientist (1882-1970)

Love is hate, war is peace, no is yes, and we're all free.

Tracy Chapman, American Singer-songwriter (b.1964)

101

Sports plays a societal role in engendering jingoist and chauvinist attitudes. They're designed to organize a community to be committed to their gladiators.

Noam Chomsky, American Author (b.1928)

Until we have the courage to recognize cruelty for what it is — whether its victim is human or animal — we cannot expect things to be much better in this world... We cannot have peace among men whose hearts delight in killing any living creature. By every act that glorifies or even tolerates such moronic delight in killing we set back the progress of humanity.

Rachel Carson, American Environmentalist (1907-1964)

Bullets cannot be recalled. They cannot be uninvented. But they can be taken out of the gun.

Martin Amis, British Author (b.1949)

Each person has inside a basic decency and goodness. If he listens to it and acts on it, he is giving a great deal of what it is the world needs most. It is not complicated but it takes courage. It takes courage for a person to listen to his own goodness and act on it.

Pablo Casals, Spanish Cellist (1876-1973)

Non-violence, which is the quality of the heart, cannot come by an appeal to the brain.

Cesar Chavez, American Union Organizer (1927-1993)

After all, a week ago, there were — Yasser Arafat was boarded up in his building in Ramallah, a building full of, evidently, German peace protestors and all kinds of people. They're now out. He's now free to show leadership, to lead the world.

George W. Bush, American President (b.1946)

I don't need your civil war, it feeds the rich and buries the poor. *Civil War.*
> Guns and Roses, American Rock Band

The most potent weapon in the hands of the oppressor is the mind of the oppressed.
> Stephen Biko, South African Activist (1946-1977)

Let us not use bombs and guns to overcome the world. Let us use love and compassion. Peace begins with a smile — smile five times a day to someone you don't really want to smile at all — do it for peace. So let us radiate the peace of God and so light his light.
> Mother Teresa, Macedonian Nun (1910-1997)

I don't wanna die in a nuclear war, I want to sail away to a distant shore, and make like an apeman. *Apeman.*
> The Kinks, British Rock Band

I have no choice. I'm a little man, a citizen, one of the people, but I'll do what I have to.
> Imprisoned in Israel for revealing nuclear secrets in1987
> Mordechai Vanunu, Moroccan Scientist (b.1954)

Courage is what it takes to stand up and speak. Courage is also what it takes to sit down and listen.
> Septima Poinsette Clark, American Civil Rights Leader
> (1898-1990)

War is not the answer, because only love can conquer hate.*What's Going On.* (1971)
> Marvin Gaye, American Singer-songwriter (1939-1984)

Teach peace, not war.
> Bradley L. Winch, American Author

If you want to make peace, you don't talk to your friends. You talk to your enemies.
> Moshe Dayan, Israeli General (1915-1981)

Very few people chose war. They chose selfishness and the result was war. Each of us, individually and nationally, must choose: total love or total war.
> Dave Dellinger, American Peace Activist (b.1916)

Women prevent the threads of life from being broken. The finest minds have always understood the peacemaking role of women.
> Mikhail S. Gorbachev, Russian Premier (b.1931)

The pursuit of peace and progress cannot end in a few years in either victory or defeat. The pursuit of peace and progress, with its trials and errors, its successes and setbacks, can never be relaxed and never abandoned.
> Dag Hammarskjold, Swedish
> Secretary General of the UN (1905-1961)

My trip to Asia begins here in Japan for an important reason. It begins here because for a century and a half now, America and Japan have formed one of the great and enduring alliances of modern times. From that alliance has come an era of peace in the Pacific.
Who forgot about something called World War II, 2002
> George W. Bush, American President (b.1946)

What the world needs now is love, sweet love. It's the only thing that there is just too little of.
*What The World Needs Now Is Love Sweet Love.*
> Jackie Del Shannon; Dionne Warwick

It is in the shelter of each other that the people live.
> Irish Proverb

To save one life, it is as if you had saved the world.

Talmud

The peace process we all aim for will not necessarily be a result of the mere signing of a treaty or agreement. It must become a matter of our everyday lives, so that peace settles and lasts and becomes supported by everybody. We therefore have to give peace all the required care and preserve it and promote it.

King Hassan II, Moroccan Monarch (1929-1999)

I believe in compulsory cannibalism. If people were forced to eat what they killed there would be no more war.

Abbie Hoffman, American Peace Acvitist (1936-1989)

Nonviolence is the supreme law of life.

Indian Proverb

I assured the prime minister, my administration will work hard to lay the foundation of peace in the Middle East — to work with our nations in the Middle East, give peace a chance. Secondly, I told him that our nation will not try to force peace, that we'll facilitate peace and that we will work with those responsible for a peace.

Referring to Ariel Sharon
George W. Bush, American President (b.1946)

The point of nonviolence is to build a floor, a strong new floor, beneath which we can no longer sink. A platform which stands a few feet above napalm, torture, exploitation, poison gas, A and H bombs, the works. Give man a decent place to stand.

Joan Baez, American Folk Singer (b.1941)

The Great Society: Bombs, Bullets and Bullshit.

American Hippy Proverb

... the wrong war in the wrong place at the wrong time against the wrong enemy.

Peter Kilfoyle, British Politician (b.1944)

The first principle of non-violent action is that of non-cooperation with everything humiliating.

Cesar Chavez, American Union Organizer (1927-1993)

Forgiveness is an inner correction that lightens the heart. It is for our peace of mind first. Being at peace, we will now have peace to give to others, and this is the most permanent and valuable gift we can possibly give.

Gerald Jampolsky, American Psychiatrist (b.1933)

Sensitivity to the immense needs of humanity brings with it a spontaneous rejection of the arms race, which is incompatible with the all out struggle against hunger, sickness, under-development and illiteracy.

John Paul II, Polish Pope (b.1920)

If we have no peace, it is because we have forgotten that we belong to each other.

Mother Teresa, Macedonion Nun (1910-1997)

There is a certain kind of peace that is not merely the absence of war. It is larger than that. The peace I am thinking of is not at the mercy of history's rule, nor is it a passive surrender to the status quo. The peace I am thinking of is the dance of an open mind when it engages another equally open one — an activity that occurs most naturally, most often in the reading & writing world we live in. Accessible as it is, this particular kind of peace warrants vigilance. *The Dancing Mind,* (1996)

Toni Morrison, American Author (b.1931)

When men talk about defense, they always claim to be protecting women and children, but they never ask the women and children what they think.

Pat Schroeder, American Politician (b.1940)

Mine is the first generation able to contemplate the possibility that we may live our entire lives without going to war or sending our children to war.

Speech at the NATO-Russia Summit, May,1997
Tony Blair, British Prime Minister (b.1953)

Let's roll for justice, let's roll for truth. Let's not let our children grow up fearful in their youth. *Let's Roll.*

Neil Young, Canadian Singer-songwriter (b.1945)

Yes, we love peace, but we are not willing to take wounds for it, as we are for war.

John Andrew Holmes

The non-violent technique does not depend for its success on the goodwill of the oppressor, but rather on the unfailing assistance of God.

Cesar Chavez, American Union Organizer (1927-1993)

You measure peace with guns, progress in megatons. Who's left when the war is won? *Soldier Of Plenty.*

Jackson Browne, American Singer-songwriter (b.1948)

Lead me from death to life, from falsehood to truth;
Lead me from despair to hope, from fear to trust;
Lead me from hate to love, from war to peace;
Let peace fill our heart, our world, our universe.
*Prayer for Peace.*

Satish Kumar, Indian Peace Activist (b.1936)

The real differences around the world today are not between Jews and Arabs; Protestants and Catholics; Muslims, Croats, and Serbs. The real differences are between those who embrace peace and those who would destroy it; between those who look to the future and those who cling to the past; between those who open their arms and those who are determined to clench their fists.

Bill Clinton, American President (b.1946)

And they shall beat their swords into plowshares, and their spears into pruninghooks: nation shall not lift up sword against nation, neither shall they learn war any more.

Bible: Isaiah 2:4

The abolition of war, far from being a Utopian dream, is a realistic objective for leaders and citizens alike.

Report of the 27th Party Congress, USSR 1989

The pacifist's task today is to find a method of helping and healing which provides a revolutionary constructive substitute for war.

Vera Brittain, British Author (1893-1970)

Non-violence exacts a very high price from one who practices it. But once you are able to meet that demand then you can do most things.

Cesar Chavez, American Union Organizer (1927-1993)

If you want to make peace with your enemy, you have to work with your enemy. Then he becomes your partner.

Nelson Mandela, South African Prime Minister (b.1918)

Never doubt that a small group of thoughtful committed citizens can change the world: Indeed it's the only thing that ever has.

Margaret Mead, American Anthropologist (1901-1978)

The sad truth is that most evil is done by people who never make up their minds to be good or evil.

Hannah Arendt, German-born American Philosopher (1906-1975)

There is no such thing as defeat in non-violence.

Cesar Chavez, American Union Organizer (1927-1993)

Nonviolence doesn't always work — but violence never does.

Madge Michaels-Cyrus

We've got pockets of persistent poverty in our society, which I refuse to declare defeat — I mean, I refuse to allow them to continue on. And so one of the things that we're trying to do is to encourage a faith-based initiative to spread its wings all across America, to be able to capture this great compassionate spirit.

George W. Bush, American President (b.1946)

Conflict is inevitable, but combat is optional.

Max Lucade

Peace is not the product of a victory or a command. It has no finishing line, no final deadline, no fixed definition of achievement. Peace is a never-ending process, the work of many decisions.

Oscar Arias Sanchez, Costa Rician Politician (b.1941)

All we are saying is: give peace a chance.

John Lennon, British Musician (1940-1980)

I believe in the religion of Islam. I believe in Allah and peace.

Muhammad Ali, American Boxer (b.1942)

Cinema simulated life, ill drama, Fourth Reich culture, Americana. Chained to the dream they got you searchin' for, the thin line between entertainment and war.
*No Shelter.*

Rage Against the Machine, American Rock Band

I do not believe in using women in combat, because females are too fierce.

Margaret Mead, American Anthropologist (1901-1978)

I swore never to be silent whenever human beings endure suffering and humiliation. We must always take sides. Neutrality helps the oppressor, never the victim. Silence encourages the tormentor, never the tormented.

Elie Weisel, Transylvanian-born American Author
(b.1928)

Jokes are better than war. Even the most aggressive jokes are better than the least aggressive wars. Even the longest jokes are better than the shortest wars.

George Mikes, Hungarian Author (1912-1987)

One little person, giving all of her time to peace, makes news. Many people, giving some of their time, can make history.

Peace Pilgrim

Nuclear war is inevitable, says the pessimists; Nuclear war is impossible, says the optimists; Nuclear war is inevitable unless we make it impossible, says the realists.

Sydney J. Harris, American Journalist (1917-1986)

One cannot subdue a man by holding back his hands. Lasting peace comes not from force.

David Borenstein

I believe that for peace a man may, even should, do everything in his power. Nothing in this world could rank higher than peace.

Anwar al-Sadat, Egyptian President (1918-1981)

Non-violence is a very powerful weapon. Most people don't understand the power of non-violence and tend to be amazed by the whole idea.Those who have been involved in bringing about change and see the difference between violence and non-violence are firmly committed to a lifetime of non-violence, not because it is easy or because it is cowardly, but because it is an effective and very powerful way.

Cesar Chavez, American Union Organizer (1927-1993)

Life only demands from you the strength you possess. Only one feat is possible- not to have to run away.

Dag Hammarskjold, Swedish
Secretary General of the UN (1905-1961)

There are no warlike people, just warlike leaders.

Ralph Bunche, American Politician (1904-1971)

We must have research for peace ... It would embrace the outstanding problems of morality. The time has come for man's intellect, his scientific method, to win over the immoral brutality and irrationality of war and militarism. Now we are forced to eliminate from the world forever this vestige of prehistoric barbarism, this curse to the human race.

Linus Pauling, American Scientist (1901-1994)

111

The suicide bombings have increased. There's too many of 'em.

George W. Bush, American President (b.1946)

I have never once been persuaded as to the causal link between the Iraqi regime, al-Qaeda and September 11. I do believe the impact of war under these circumstances is bound to weaken the international coalition against terrorism itself.

Charles Kennedy, British Politician (b.1959)

Nobody was born nonviolent. No one was born charitable. None of us comes to these things by nature but only by conversion. The first duty of the nonviolent community is helping its members work upon themselves and come to conversion.

Lanza del Vasto, French Author (1901-1981)

Gandhi once declared that it was his wife who unwittingly taught him the effectiveness of nonviolence. Who better than women should know that battles can be won without resort to physical strength? Who better than we should know all the power that resides in noncooperation?

Barbara Deming, American Author (1917-1984)

The arms race can kill, though the weapons themselves may never be used... by their cost alone, armaments kill the poor by causing them to starve.

Vatican statement to the U.N in 1976

It doesn't take a military genius to see we'll all be crispy critters after World War III. *Happy Birthday.*

Weird Al Yankovic, American Singer-songwriter

For everything there is a season,
And a time for every matter under heaven:
A time to be born, and a time to die;
A time to plant, and a time to pluck up what
    is planted;
A time to kill, and a time to heal;
A time to break down, and a time to build up;
A time to weep, and a time to laugh;
A time to mourn, and a time to dance;
A time to throw away stones, And a time to
    gather stones together;
A time to embrace, And a time to refrain
    from embracing;
A time to seek, and a time to lose;
A time to keep, and a time to throw away;
A time to tear, and a time to sew;
A time to keep silence, and a time to speak;
A time to love, and a time to hate,
A time for war, and a time for peace.

               Bible: Ecclesiastes 3:1-8

In 1989, thirteen nations comprising 1,695,000 people experienced nonviolent revolutions that succeeded beyond anyone's wildest expectations ... If we add all the countries touched by major nonviolent actions in our century (the Philippines, South Africa ... the independence movement in India ... ) the figure reaches 3,337, 400,000, a staggering 65% of humanity! All this in the teeth of the assertion, endlessly repeated, that nonviolence doesn't work in the 'real' world.

               Walter Wink, American Author

You don't have to have fought in a war to love peace.
      Geraldine A. Ferraro, American Politician (b.1935)

We call for:"...renunciation by the nuclear powers of war — both nuclear and conventional — against each other or against third countries..."
Biennial Report, U.S. Institute of Peace 1986

You know, if people are not pacifists, it's not their fault. It's because society puts them in that spot. You've got to change it. You don't just change a man — you've got to change his environment as you do it.
Cesar Chavez, American Union Organizer (1927-1993)

Looking for peace is like looking for a turtle with a mustache: You won't be able to find it. But when your heart is ready, peace will come looking for you.
*Reflections*
Ajahn Chah, Thailandese Buddhist Monk (1918-1992)

It is my strong conviction that the responsibility for dis-disarming Iraq should rest with the United Nations. As a matter of conscience I question the United States government 's apparent intention to commence war in Iraq.
Youssou N'Dour, Senegalese Musician (b.1959)

Our future on this planet, exposed as it is to nuclear annihilation, depends on one single factor: humanity must make a moral about-face.
John Paul II, Polish Pope (b.1920)

Peace with a club in hand is war.
Portuguese Proverb

Why is it so easy for us to be willing to pick up arms and risk our lives, and so difficult to put down those same weapons and still risk our lives — in the cause of life?
Ramzi Kysia, American-Muslim, Peace Activist

The master's tools will never destroy the master's house. *Sister Outsider.*
> Audre Lorde, American Poet (1934-1992)

The greatest disease in the West today is not TB or leprosy; it is being unwanted, unloved, and uncared for. We can cure physical diseases with medicine, but the only cure for loneliness, despair, and hopelessness is love. There are many in the world who are dying for a piece of bread but there are many more dying for a little love. The poverty in the West is a different kind of poverty — it is not only a poverty of loneliness but also of spirituality. There's a hunger for love, as there is a hunger for God.
> Mother Teresa, Macedonian Nun (1910-1997)

One can always win a war, but how does one conquer peace?
> Michael Holmboe Meyer, Norweigan Author (b.1952)

There is no way to peace.
Peace is the way.
> A.J. Muste, Dutch-born
> American Politcian
> (1885-1967)

If in our daily life we can smile, if we can be peaceful and happy, not only we, but everyone will profit from it. This is the most basic kind of peace work.
> Thich Nhat Hanh, Vietnamese Poet (b.1926)

War ends nothing.
> African Proverb

115

God has made of one blood all nations under heaven. No man can suddenly become my enemy just because he happened to have been born on the other side of a river or a boundary line, and his government has issued an ultimatum against mine. Is it not time that we refused to fight?
> Muriel Lester, British Pacifist (1884-1968)

The greatest honor history can bestow is that of peace.
> U. Thant, Burmese, Secretary General of the UN
> (1909-1974)

Peace is no more than a dream as long as we need the comfort of the clan.
> Peter Nicols, British Playwright (b.1927)

Since wars begin in the minds of men, it is in the minds of men that the defenses of peace must be constructed.
> UNESCO Statement

Everyone and everything is at war, making my poetic expression hardcore. *REALITY*
> KRS-One, American Rock Band

If there is to be any peace it will come through being, not having.
> Henry Miller, American Author (1891-1980)

Non-violence is not inaction. It is not discussion. It is not for the timid or weak... Non-violence is hard work. It is the willingness to sacrifice. It is the patience to win.
> Cesar Chavez, American Union Organizer (1927-1993)

We overturned a government without breaking a window.
> Lech Walesa, Polish Labour Organizer (b.1943)

One of the most basic principles for making and keeping peace within and between nations ... is that in political, military, moral, and spiritual confrontations, there should be an honest attempt at the reconciliation of differences before resorting to combat.

Jimmy Carter, American President (b.1924)

The more we sweat in peace the less we bleed in war.

Vijaya Lakshmi Pandit, Indian Politcian (1900-1990)

You may call for peace as loudly as you wish, but where there is no brotherhood there can in the end be no peace.

Max Lerner, American Journalist (1902-1992)

In 1984 the United States Congress establishes the University of Peace to explore non-violent conflict resolution among nations.

Pax: peace, but what a strange peace, made of unremitting toil and effort, seldom with a seen result; subject to constant interruptions, unexpected demands, short sleep at night, little comfort, sometimes scant food; beset with disappointments and usually misunderstood; yet peace all the same, undeviating, filled with joy and gratitude and love.

Rumer Godden, British Author (1907-1998)

If we do not change our direction we are likely to end up where we are headed for.

Chinese Proverb

The most terrifying monster lurking in the darkness of Hiroshima is precisely the possibility that man might become no longer human.

Kenzaburo Oe, Japanese Author (b.1935)

117

Lord. But "If your enemies are hungry, feed them; if they are thirsty, give them something to drink; by doing this you will heap burning coals upon their heads." Do not be conquered by evil but conquer evil with good.

Bible: Romans 12:14-21

I come into the peace of wild things who do not tax their lives with forethought of grief... For a time I rest in the grace of the world, and am free.

Wendell Berry, American Poet (b.1924)

Peace is more precious than a piece of land.

Anwar al-Sadat, Egyptian President (1918-1981)

Lead me from death to life, from falsehood to truth; Lead me from despair to hope, from fear to trust; Lead me from hate to love, from war to peace; Let peace fill our heart, our world, our universe.

Satish Kumar, Indian Mystic (b.1947)

How can one not speak about war, poverty, and inequality when people who suffer from these afflictions don't have a voice to speak?

Isabel Allende, Peruvian Author (b.1942)

I take it that what all men are really after is some form of, perhaps only some formula of, peace.

James Conrad

When you're finally up on the moon, looking back at the earth, all these differences and nationalistic traits are pretty well going to blend and you're going to get a concept that maybe this is really one world and why the hell can't we learn to live together like decent people?

Frank Borman, American Astronaut (b.1928)

118

If you want to make the world a better place, take a look at yourself, and make a change.
*Man In The Mirror,*
   Michael Jackson, American Singer-songwriter (b.1955)

If you want peace, work for justice.
   Paul VI, Italian Pope (1897-1978)

For peace of mind, we need to resign as general manager of the universe.
   Larry Eisenberg, American Author (b.1919)

You don't make peace with friends. You make it with very unsavory enemies.
   Yitzhak Rabin, Israeli Prime Minister (1922-1995)

The universities have prostituted themselves, using their skilled personnel to work for death and not life.
   Helen Caldicott, Australian Environmentalist (b.1938)

To be at one with God is to be at peace... peace is to be found only within, and unless one finds it there he will never find it at all. Peace lies not in the external world. It lies within one's own soul.
   Ralph W. Trine, American Author

The Russians feared Ike. They didn't fear me.
   Lyndon B. Johnson, American President (1908-1973)

We shall be Canadians first, foremost, and always, and our policies will be decided in Canada and not dictated by any other country.
   John Diefenbaker, Canadian Prime Minister
(1897-1972)

Smiling is very important. If we are not able to smile, then the world will not have peace. It is not by going out for a demonstration against nuclear missiles that we can bring about peace. It is with our capacity of smiling, breathing, and being at peace that we can make peace.
Thich Nhat Hanh, Vietnamese Poet (b.1926)

This is my commandment, that ye love one another.
Bible: John 15:12

Aggressive conduct, if allowed to go unchecked and unchallenged, ultimately leads to war.
John F. Kennedy, American President (1917-1963)

War is over, if you want it. *Happy Xmas, War Is Over.*
John Lennon, British Singer-songwriter (1940-1980)

As this long and difficult war ends, I would like to address a few special words to the American people: Your steadfastness in supporting our insistence on peace with honor has made peace with honor possible.
Richard M. Nixon, American President (1913-1994)

I went to Vietnam to wage war,
in order that there would be peace,
but there was no peace,
only much death and sorrow.
And I only hope that from the knowledge
of those who have returned,
those who will return,
and those who will not return,
that there will never be a war in our own country.
Sp4 Mayo, Chu Lai, South Vietnam, Dec 1970

Every night, whisper *peace* in your husband's ear.
Andrei A. Gromyko, Russian Politician (1909-1989)

120

Back when the country was strong, back before Elvis and before the Vietnam war came along. *Are The Good Times Really Over For Good.*
Merle Haggard, American, Singer-songwriter (b.1937)

The ultimate measure of a person is not where one stands in moments of comfort and convenience, but where one stands in times of challenge and controversy.
Martin Luther King Jr, American Civil Rights Leader (1929-1968)

Peace is the deliberate adjustment of my life to the will of God.
Anonymous

The first question which the priest and the Levite asked [on the Jericho Road] was: 'If I stop to help this man, what will happen to me?' But ... the good Samaritan reversed the question: 'If I do not stop to help this man, what will happen to him?'
Martin Luther King Jr, American Civil Rights Leader (1929-1968)

The ultimate test of a nation's character is not how it responds to adversity in war but how it meets the challenge of peace. *Beyond Peace,* (1994)
Richard M. Nixon, American President (1913-1994)

Compromise does not mean cowardice.
John F. Kennedy, American President (1917-1963)

The life of inner peace, being harmonious and without stress, is the easiest type of existence.
Norman Vincent Peale, American Author (1898-1993)

I am so excited about Canadians ruling the world.
John Diefenbaker, Canadian Prime Minister
(1897-1972)

In 1981 the United Nations establishes the University of Peace in Costa Rica.

Injustice anywhere is a threat to justice everywhere. We are caught in an inescapable network of mutuality, tied in a single garment of destiny.
Martin Luther King Jr, American Civil Rights Leader
(1929-1968)

When the power of love overcomes the love of power the world will know peace.
Jimi Hendrix, American Musician (1942-1970)

The greatest honor history can bestow is that of Peacemaker.
Richard M. Nixon, American President (1913-1994)

I made an unauthorized separate peace with the enemy. I was going to find a way to quit killing.
*The War Lover*, (1959)
John Hersey, American Author (1914-1993)

Democracy don't rule the world. You'd better get that in your head; This world is ruled by violence, But I guess that's better left unsaid.
Bob Dylan, American Singer-songwriter (b.1941)

Millions of mind guerrillas, raising the spirit of peace and love, not war. *Mind Games.*
John Lennon, British Singer-songwriter (1940-1980)

The Peace Corps is a sort of Howard Johnson's on the main drag into maturity.

> Paul Theroux, American Author (b.1941)

It isn't enough to talk about peace. One must believe in it. And it isn't enough to believe in it. One must work at it.

> Eleanor Roosevelt, American Diplomat (1884-1962)

We are advocates of the abolition of war, we do not want war; but war can only be abolished through war, and in order to get rid of the gun it is necessary to take up the gun.

> Mao Tse-Tung, Chinese Chairman (1893-1976)

Only when there are many people who are pools of peace, silence, understanding, will war disappear.

> Bhagwan Shree Rajneesh (Osho) Indian (1931-1990)

The means by which we live have outdistanced the ends for which we live. Our scientific power has outrun our spiritual power. We have guided missiles and misguided men.

> Martin Luther King Jr, American Civil Rights Leader
> (1929-1968)

Poetry is an act of peace. Peace goes into the making of a poet as flour goes into the making of bread. *Memoirs*

> Pablo Neruda, Chilian Author (1904-1973)

It is My own peace I give unto you. Not, notice, the world's peace.

> Rumer Godden, British Author (1907-1998)

Those who make peaceful revolution impossible will make violent revolution inevitable.

> John F. Kennedy, American President (1917-1963)

Aspiring sincerely to an international peace based on justice and order, the Japanese people forever renounce war as a sovereign right of the nation. Article IX
New Constitution of Japan, 1947

Then said Jesus unto him, Put up again thy sword into his place: for all they that take the sword shall perish with the sword.
Bible: Matthew 26:5-2

War is Good for Business. Invest Your Son.
Poster by Seymour Chwast

If it were proved to me that in making war, my ideal had a chance of being realized, I would still say "No" to war. For one does not create human society on mounds of corpses.
Louis Lecoin, French Pacifist (1888-1971)

In 1970 a treaty with the USSR, Germany pledges the renunciation of force to achieve political ends.
New Hampshire Peace Action Organization

I'd like someone to mention the day that Martin Luther King, Jr., tried to give his life serving others. I'd like somebody to say that day, that Martin Luther King tried to love somebody. I want you to say that day, that I tried to be right on the war question. I want you to be able to say that day, that I did try to feed the hungry ... I want you to say that I tried to love and serve humanity. Yes, if you want to say that I was a drum major, say that I was a drum major for justice; say that I was a drum major for peace; I was a drum major for righteousness ... I want to leave a committed life behind.
Martin Luther King Jr, American Civil Rights Leader
(1929-1968)

Curtis Le May wants to bomb Hanoi and Haiphong. You know how he likes to go around bombing.
Lyndon B. Johnson, American President (1908-1973)

This is something that I cherish. Once in a friend's home I came across this blessing, and took it down in shorthand ... it says something I like to live with: "Oh Thou, who dwellest in so many homes, possess Thyself of this. Bless the life that is sheltered here. Grant that trust and peace and comfort abide within, and that love and life and usefulness may go out from this home forever.
Claudia (Ladybird) Alta Taylor Johnson (b.1912)

Every day we do things, we are things that have to do with peace. If we are aware of our life..., our way of looking at things, we will know how to make peace right in the moment, we are alive.
Thich Nhat Hanh, Vietnamese Poet (b.1926)

Imagine all the people living life in peace. You may say I'm a dreamer, but I'm not the only one. I hope someday you'll join us, and the world will live as one.
John Lennon, British Musician (1940-1980)

Find those little islands of grace during the day in which you can interiorize peace and reverence for life. Become an emmissary for peace, reverence and compassion by your own example. In sanctuary it is much easier to get in touch with these soulful qualities, and thereby share them as gifts with others. Let your own commitment to find sacred time and space be the spiritual beacon that draws others to the safe harbor of their own unique form of sanctuary.
Christopher Forrest McDowell

One day we shall win freedom, but not only for ourselves. We shall so appeal to your heart and conscience that we shall win you in the process, and our victory will be a double victory.

Martin Luther King Jr, American Civil Rights Leader
(1929-1968)

I asked how an idea, a philosophy, or a religion, could be eternally true if it changed its nature according to the temporal activities and policies of men. It seemed to me irrational to expect to overcome these world evils by killing each other's wives and children. This generation, though liking to appear hard-boiled and realist, was being naive, romantic, unscientific.

Muriel Lester, British Pacifist (1884-1968)

When you find peace within yourself, you become the kind of person who can live at peace with others.

Peace Pilgrim

I'm not very keen for doves or hawks. I think we need more owls.

George D. Aiken, American Politician (1892-1984

Through Gandhi and my own life experience, I have learned about nonviolence. I believe that human life is a very special gift from God, and that no one has a right to take that away in any cause, however just. I am convinced that nonviolence is more powerful than violence.

Cesar Chavez, American Union Organizer (1927-1993)

If everyone demanded peace instead of another television set, then there'd be peace.

John Lennon, British Musician (1940-1980)

War is as outmoded as cannibalism, chattel slavery, blood-feuds and dueling — an insult to God and man — a daily crucifixion of Christ.

Muriel Lester, British Pacifist (1884-1968)

Peace is not merely a distant goal that we seek, but a means by which we arrive at that goal.

Martin Luther King Jr, American Civil Rights Leader (1929-1968)

Compassion is sometimes the fatal capacity for feeling what it is like to live inside somebody else's skin. It is the knowledge that there can never really be any peace and joy for me until there is peace and joy finally for you too.

Frederick Buechner, American Clergyman (b.1926)

To be nobody but yourself in a world which is doing its best day and night to make you everybody else, means to fight the hardest battle which any human being can fight, and never stop fighting.

E. E. Cummings, American Poet (1864-1962)

If you succumb to the temptation of using violence in the struggle, unborn generations will be the recipients of a long and desolate night of bitterness, and your chief legacy to the future will be an endless reign of meaningless chaos.

Martin Luther King Jr, American Civil Rights Leader (1929-1968)

We all say no to war, we are all for justice and peace. But sometimes in order to maintain peace, armed action is necessary. But we hope it won't be the case.

Silvio Berlusconi, Italian Prime Minister (b.1926)

If the Nazis have really been guilty of the unspeakable crimes circumstantially imputed to them, then — let us make no mistake — pacifism is faced with a situation with which it cannot cope. The conventional pacifist conception of a reasonable or generous peace is irrelevant to this reality.
John Middleton Murry, British Author (1889-2002

Until you make peace with who you are, you'll never be content with what you have.
Doris Mortman, American Author

Peace is a never ending process. It cannot ignore our differences or overlook our common interests. It requires us to work and live together.
Oscar Arias Sanchez, Costa Rican Politician (b.1941)

The hippies wanted peace and love. We wanted Ferraris, blondes and switchblades.
Alice Cooper, American Musician (b.1948)

Peace is not a passive but an active condition, not a negation but an affirmation. It is a gesture as strong as war.
Mary Roberts Rinehart, American Author (1876-1958)

If I were the king of the world, tell you what I'd do. I'd throw away the cars and the bars and the wars, and make sweet love to you. *Joy To The World.*
Three Dog Night, American Rock Band

Softer is stronger than hard, water than rock, love than violence.
Herman Hesse, German Author (1877-1962)

I believe that unarmed truth and unconditional love will have the final word in reality. That is why right, temporarily defeated, is stronger than evil triumphant.
Martin Luther King Jr, American Civil Rights Leader (1929-1968)

If a man would live in peace he should be blind, deaf, and dumb.
Turkish Proverb

But peace does not rest in the charters and covenants alone. It lies in the hearts and minds of all people. So let us not rest all our hopes on parchment and on paper, let us strive to build peace, a desire for peace, a willingness to work for peace in the hearts and minds of all of our people. I believe that we can. I believe the problems of human destiny are not beyond the reach of human beings.
John F. Kennedy, American President (1917-1963)

...nation shall not lift up up sword against nation, neither shall they learn war any more.
Bible: Micah 4:3

I do not want the peace which passeth understanding, I want the understanding which bringeth peace.
Helen Keller, American Educator (1880-1968)

Peace is only possible if men cease to place their happiness in the possession of things "which cannot be shared," and if they raise themselves to a point where they adopt an abstract principle superior to their egotisms. In other words, it can only be obtained by a betterment of human morality.
Julien Benda, French Philosopher (1867-1956)

Every nation sincerely desires peace; and all nations pursue courses which if persisted in, must make peace impossible.

Sir Norman Angell, British Author (1872-1967)

In every child who is born, no matter what circumstances, and of no matter what parents, the potentiality of the human race is born again: and in him, too, once more, and of each of us, our terrific responsibility toward human life; toward the utmost idea of goodness, of the horror of terror, and of God.

James Agee, American Journalist (1909-1955)

If you see good in people, you radiate a harmonious loving energy which uplifts those who are around you. If you can maintain this habit, this energy will turn into a steady flow of love.

Annamalai Swami, Indian Spiritual Teacher (1906-1995)

Everything else can wait but the search for God cannot wait, and love one another.

George Harrison, British Musician (1943-2001)

Anger is an acid that can do more harm to the vessel in which it stands than to anything on which it is poured.

Anonymous

I plan to stand by nonviolence, because I have found it to be a philosophy of life that regulates not only my dealings in the struggle for racial justice, but also my dealings with people, and with my own self.

Martin Luther King Jr, American Civil Rights Leader (1929-1968)

They make a desert and call it peace

Talmud

130

Peace is an environment where conflicts are resolved without violence, where people are free, not exploited, living so they can grow to their full potential.
Gerard Vanderhaar, American Professor (b.1930)

In the struggle rewards are few. In fact, I know of only two, loving friends and living dreams. These rewards are not so few it seems.
Anonymous

Peace is not the product of a victory or a command. It has no finishing line, no final deadline, no fixed definition of achievement. Peace is a never-ending process, the work of many decisions.
Oscar Arias Sanchez, Costa Rican Politician (b1941)

You'll never find peace of mind until you listen to your heart.
George Michael, British Singer-songwriter (b.1963)

In History, stagnant waters, whether they be the stagnant waters of custom or those of despotism, harbour no life; life is dependent on the ripples created by a few eccentric individuals. In homage to that life & vitality, the community has to brave certain perils and must countenance a measure of heresy. One must live dangerously if one wants to live at all.
Herbert Read, British Author (1893-1968)

Nonviolence means avoiding not only external physical violence but also internal violence of spirit. You not only refuse to shoot a man, but you refuse to hate him.
Martin Luther King Jr, American Civil Rights Leader (1929-1968)

131

Get up, stand up, stand up for your rights. Get up, stand up, don't give up the fight. *Get Up, Stand Up.*
Bob Marley, Jamaican Singer-songwriter (1929-1968)

In 1966 the United States Congress establishes the Peace Corps with 10,000 active volunteers in 52 countries.
New Hampshire Peace Action Organization

In India when we meet and part we often say, "Namaste," which means: I honor the place in you where the entire universe resides; I honor the place in you of love, of light, of truth, of peace. I honor the place within you where if you are in that place in you and I am in that place in me, there is only one of us ... "Namaste."
Ram Dass (Richard Elpert) American Author (b.1933)

Any intelligent fool can make things bigger, more complex, and more violent. It takes a touch of genius — and a lot of courage — to move in the opposite direction.
E. F. Schumacher, German Author (b.1911)

The love of one's country is a splendid thing. But why should love stop at the border?
Pablo Casals, Spanish Cellist (1876-1973)

All I want is peace and love on this planet, ain't that how God planned it? *Fear Of The Black Planet.*
Public Enemy, America Rock Band

We plant seeds that will flower as results in our lives, so best to remove the weeds of anger, avarice, envy and doubt, that peace and abundance may manifest for all.
Dorothy Day, American Journalist (b.1933)

We can't become nonviolent on the basis of intellectual conviction. Commitment to nonviolence demands a very profound conversion of mind and heart. If we take the time to pray with Jesus, we too will be converted in mind and heart. It won't work if we try to reason it out. The only way is through a change of heart, a coming into a way of being that is the way of Jesus.
Thomas Gumbleton, American Catholic Bishop (b.1930)

The two kinds of people who exist in this world [at any one time] are the decent and the indecent. Color, religion and nationality are irrelevant. Kindness, decency and behavior are what matters most. Our collective challenge, it seems, is to create a city and community where decent people of all races, ethnicities and religions can look into the faces of other decent people and see only one thing — God's image smiling back.
Micah Greenstein, American Rabbi (b.1952)

The liberated woman is not that modern doll who wears make-up and tasteless clothes ... The liberated woman is a person who believes that she is as human as a man. The liberated woman does not insist on her freedom so as to abuse it.
Ghada Samman,
Syrian Author (b.1942)

Pity the planet, all joy gone
from this sweet volcanic cone;
peace to our children when they fall
in small war on the heels of small war.
Robert Traill Spence Lowell, American Poet(1917-1977)

Reconciliation should be accompanied by justice, otherwise it will not last. While we all hope for peace it shouldn't be peace at any cost but peace based on principle, on justice.

Corazon Aquino, President of the Philippines (b.1933)

The EU have been pathetic and appalling. I thought we had dealt with that 20 years ago when the electorate of our countries said never again.

Referring to the impending famine in Somali in 2003
Bob Geldof, Irish Singer-songwriter (b.1954)

It is beyond me how any human being can be a proud national — uncritical — when we consider the many crimes each and every nation has on its conscience. Besides, the nation-state is no longer the appropriate unit for a humanity more and more interlocked in communication, in commerce and in global menaces. It is today about as out-of-date as was the castle in the First World War.

Sir Yehudi Menuhin, American-born British Musician
(1916-1999)

Security is mostly a superstition. It does not exist in nature, nor do the children of humans as a whole experience it. Avoiding danger is not safer in the long run than outright exposure. Life is either a daring adventure, or nothing.

Helen Keller, American Teacher (1880-1968)

Productive work, love and thought are possible only if a person can be, when necessary, quiet and alone. To be able to listen to oneself is the necessary condition for relating oneself to others.

Erich Fromm, German Psychiatrist (1900-1980)

Hitler and Mussolini were only the primary spokesmen for the attitude of domination and craving for power that are in the heart of almost everyone. Until the source is cleared, there will always be confusion and hate, wars and class antagonisms.
J. Krishnamurti, Indian Spiritual Leader (1895-1986)

If we could raise one generation with unconditional love, there would be no Hitlers. We need to teach the next generation of children from Day One that they are responsible for their lives. Mankind's greatest gift, also its greatest curse, is that we have free choice. We can make our choices built from love or from fear.
Elizabeth Kubler-Ross, Swiss-born American Psychiatrist (b.1926)

Civilization and violence are antithetical concepts.
Martin Luther King Jr, American Civil Rights Leader (1929-1968)

I've never written a political song. Songs can't save the world. I've gone through all that.
Bob Dylan, American Singer-songwriter (b.1941)

We have had enough of blood and tears. Enough!
Yitzhak Rabin, Israeli Prime Minister (1922-1995)

Our government has declared a military victory in Iraq. As a patriot, I will not celebrate. I will mourn the dead — the American GIs, and also the Iraqi dead, of which there have been many, many more. I will mourn the Iraqi children, not just those who are dead, but those who have been be blinded, crippled, disfigured, or traumatized, like the bombed children of Afghanistan who, as reported by American visitors, lost their power

of speech. The American media has not given us a full picture of the human suffering caused by our bombing; for that, we need to read the foreign press.
Howard Zinn, American Peace Activist (b.1922)

If our country is worth dying for in time of war let us resolve that it is truly worth living for in time of peace.
Hamilton Fish, American Politician (1888-1991)

The U.S. Congress passes (360-29) the Fulbright Resolution committing organizations for peace in 1943.
New Hampshire Peace Action Organization

If peace ... only had the music and pageantry of war, there'd be no wars.
Sophie Kerr, American Author (1880-1965)

A spiritual person tries less to be godly than to be deeply human.
William Sloan Coffin Jr, American Author

The God of life summons us to life; more, to be lifegivers, especially toward those who lie under the heel of the powers.
Daniel Berrigan, American Jesuit Priest (b.1921)

The only thing that's been a worse flop than the organization of nonviolence has been the organization of violence.
Joan Baez, American Folk Singer (b.1941)

Out on the edge of darkness there rides a peace train, O Peace Train take this country, come take me home again ... *Peace Train* (1971)
Yusuf Islam (Cat Stevens) British Singer-songwriter (b.1948)

August 6, 1945 is a day the Japanese will never forget. This is the day the world's first atomic bomb was dropped on the city of Hiroshima. The bomb fell from an airplane named the "Enola Gay" at 8:15 a.m. and exploded 43 seconds later, at 1,900 ft. above the city. The results were devastating. The intense heat generated from the bomb ranged from 7,200 to 10,000 degrees fahrenheit. Thousands were instantly killed, vaporized from the searing heat. Others were terribly disfigured with limbs melted from their bodies and skin peeling off in large strips. The intense heat melted the eyeballs of some who had stared in wonder at the blast. Big black flies appeared and tried to lay eggs on human flesh. The injured were so weak that they could not brush away the flies that nestled in their hands and necks." Doomsday said survivor Michiko Watanabe. Throughout the city, parents and children were discovering one another wounded or dead. "A mother, driven half-mad while looking for her child, was calling his name. At last she found him. His head looked like a boiled octopus. His eyes were half-closed, and his mouth was white, pursed, and swollen." The blast was equivalent to 12,500 tons of TNT. By present standards, the bomb was a small one, and in today's arsenals it would be classed among the merely tactical weapons. However, it was still large enough to transform a city of some 340,000 thousand people into hell in a matter of seconds. Only 6,000 buildings of the 76,000 were left undamaged; 48,000 were completely leveled. By the end of the day there were 100,000 dead. The figure would rise to 140,000 by the end of the year, due to radiation sickness and other complications.

*Hiroshima, The Nuclear Predicament,* (1986)
Jonathan Schell, American Peace Activist

You save your soul by saving someone else's body.
> Arthur Hertzberg, Russian-born American Author
> (b.1903)

A rattlesnake, if cornered will become so angry it will bite itself. That is exactly what the harboring of hate and resentment against others is — a biting of oneself. We think we are harming others in holding these spites and hates, but the deeper harm is to ourselves.
> E. Stanley Jones, American Evangelist (1884-1972)

Past the seeker as he prayed came the crippled and the beggar and the beaten. And seeing them ... he cried, "Great God, how is it that a loving creator can see such things and yet do nothing about them?"...God said, "I did do something. I made you."
> Sufi Teaching

The war photographers' fervent hope is that they become unemployed.
> Robert Capa, Hungarian Photograher (1913-1954)

It's probably better If one little old general in shirt sleeves can take Saigon, think about 200 million Chinese comin' down those trails. No sir, I don't want to fight them.
> Lyndon B. Johnson, American President (1908-1973)

We suffer from an incurable malady: Hope.
> Mahmoud Darwish, Palestinian Poet

Much violence is based on the illusion that life is a property to be defended and not to be shared.
> Henri Nouwen, Dutch Jesuit Priest (1932-1996)

The story of the human race is characterized by efforts to get along much more than by violent disputes, although it's the latter that make the history books. Violence is actually exceptional. The human race has survived because of cooperation, not aggression.

Gerard Vanderhaar, American Professor (b.1930)

All who affirm the use of violence admit it is only a means to achieve justice and peace. But peace and justice are nonviolence ... the final end of history. Those who abandon nonviolence have no sense of history. Rather they are bypassing history, freezing history, betraying history.

André Trocmé, German Pastor (b.1901)

Peace comes from being able to contribute the best that we have, and all that we are, toward creating a world that supports everyone. But it is also securing the space for others to contribute the best that they have and all that they are.

Hafsat Abiola, Nigerian Civil Rights Leader (1969-1996)

How many times must the cannonballs fly, before they're forever banned? ... How many deaths will it takes till he knows that too many people have died?

*Blowin' in the Wind,* (1962)

Bob Dylan, American Singer-songwriter (b.1941)

The job of the peacemaker is to stop war, to purify the world, to get it saved from poverty and riches, to heal the sick, to comfort the sad, to wake up those who have not yet found God, to create joy and beauty wherever you go, to find God in everything and everyone.

Muriel Lester, British Pacifist (1884-1968)

World peace is us.... We are each walking agents of the vision of peace we carry inside us.

Kathleen Vande Kieft, American Author

One is called to live nonviolently, even if the change one works for seems impossible. It may or may not be possible to turn the US around through nonviolent revolution. But one thing favors such an attempt: the total inability of violence to change anything for the better.

Daniel Berrigan, American Jesuit Priest (b.1921)

It's better to have him inside the tent pissing out, than outside the tent pissing in.

Lyndon B. Johnson, American President (1908-1973)

Thus saith the Lord, Ye shall not go up, nor fight against your brethren.

Bible: II Chronicles 11:4

Can one have love? If we could, love would need to be a thing, a substance that one can have, own, possess. The truth is, there is no such thing as "love". "Love" is an abstraction, perhaps a goddess or an alien being, although nobody has ever seen this goddess. In reality, there exists only the act of loving. To love is a productive activity. It implies caring for, knowing, responding, affirming, enjoying: the person, the tree, the painting, the idea. It means bringing to life, increasing his or her aliveness. It is a process, self-renewing and self increasing from *To Have or to Be?*

Erich Fromm, German Psychiatrist (1900-1980)

If there were more leaders like Mr. Trudeau, (Canada's Prime Minister) there would be world peace.

John Lennon, British Musician (1940-1980)

140

A man seeks to control and harmonize his life so that he may be at peace. But nature, perhaps, is not ready to round off so small a piece of creation, and he finds himself swept into conflict by impulses that are part of some large whole. There are greater issues than his comfort. A bad peace is better than a good war.

Russian proverb

A musician must make music, an artist must paint, a poet must write if he is to be ultimately at peace with himself. What one can be, one must be.

Abraham Maslow, American Psychologist (1908-1970)

If there's a God in heaven, what's he waiting for? If He can't hear the children, then he must see the war.
*If There's A God In Heaven.*

Elton John, British Singer-songwriter (b.1947)

God has made of one blood all nations under heaven. No man can suddenly become my enemy just because he happened to have been born on the other side of a river or a boundary line, and his government has issued an ultimatum against mine. Is it not time that we refused to fight?

Muriel Lester, British Pacifist (1884-1968)

I took a speed-reading course and read *War and Peace* in twenty minutes. It involves Russia.

Woody Allen, American Comedian (b.1935)

Establishing lasting peace is the work of education; all politics can do is keep us out of war.

Maria Montessori, Italian-born American Educator
(1870-1952)

Realize that true happiness lies within you. Waste no time and effort searching for peace and contentment and joy in the world outside. Remember that there is no happiness in having or in getting, but only in giving. Reach out. Share. Smile. Hug. Happiness is a perfume you cannot pour on others without getting a few drops on yourself. *The Greatest Salesman in the World* (1996.

Og Mandino, American Author

We discovered that peace at any price is no peace at all.

Eve Denise Curie, French Pianist (b.1904)

It is better we disintegrate in peace and not in pieces.

Benjamin Nnamdi Azikiwe, President of Nigeria(b.1904)

Brothers, you came from our own people. You are killing your own brothers. Any human order to kill must be subordinate to the law of God, which says, 'Thou shalt not kill'. No soldier is obliged to obey an order contrary to the law of God. No one has to obey an immoral law. It is high time you obeyed your consciences rather than sinful orders. The church cannot remain silent before such an abomination ... In the name of God, in the name of this suffering people whose cry rises to heaven more loudly each day, I implore you, I beg you, I order you: stop the repression.

Appealing to the men of the armed forces
Oscar Romero, Salvadorian Catholic Archbishop
(1917-1980)

Scientists who work for nuclear power or nuclear energy have sold their soul to the devil. They are either dumb, stupid, or highly compromised ... Free enterprise really means rich people get richer. And they have the freedom to exploit and psychologically rape their fellow human

beings in the process ... Capitalism is destroying the earth. Cuba is a wonderful country. What Castro's done is superb. *Trashing the Planet*, (1990)
Helen Caldicott, Australian Environmentalist (b.1938)

Adulterers in churches and pornography in the schools, you got gangsters in power and lawbreakers making rules. When you gonna wake up?*When You Gonna Wake Up.*
Bob Dylan, American Singer-songwriter (b.1941)

We must pursue the peace efforts as if there were no terrorism, and fight the terrorists as if there were no peace efforts.
Jacob Jakobovits, American Politician (1923-1999)

To many men... the miasma of peace seems more suffocating than the bracing air of war.
George Steiner, French-born Author (b.1929)

What a terrible thing has happened to us all! To you there, to us here, to all everywhere. Peace who was becoming bright-eyed, now sits in the shadow of death; her handsome champion has been killed as he walked by her very side. Her gallant boy is dead. What a cruel, foul, and most unnatural murder!
Letter to Mrs Rose Russell concerning JFK's death
Sean O'Casey, Irish Poet (1880-1964)

Peace is not the absence of war. Lasting peace is rooted in justice. It is rooted in a democratic culture which cherishes the rule of law and scorns the summary justice, social terrorism and gangsterism which are a fact of life for too many people in Northern Ireland.
David Trimble, Northern Irish Politician (b.1944)

In the west ... we as individuals have great liberty, but little autonomy. We have the right to determine the shape of our future, but we do not bother to avail ourselves of it very much.

> Jonathan Schell, American Peace Activist

If the principles crystalized during the Nuremberg Trials at the end of World War II were applied to allied prosecution of the Gulf War, hangings of the U.S. military brass would be in order.
*Oregonian,* (1993)

> Helen Caldicott, Australian Environmentalist (b.1938)

To me war is like an aging actress — more and more dangerous and less and less photogenic.

> Robert Capa, Hungarian Photographer (1913-1954)

If we fight a war and win it with H-bombs, what history will remember is not the ideals we were fighting for but the methods we used to accomplish them. These methods will be compared to the warfare of Genghis Khan who ruthlessly killed every last inhabitant of Persia

> Hans Albrecht Bethe, German Physicist (b.1906)

Ten years after the end of the Cold War, nuclear danger is rising. Despite the end of the struggle in whose name the great nuclear arsenals were built, Washington now seeks to stop proliferation while holding on to its own arsenal indefinitely. But as nuclear restrictions falter — battered by India's and Pakistan's tests, Iraq's defiance, North Korea's missiles, and the U.S. missile-defense plan — the absence of a middle ground becomes stark. Holding on to nuclear arms is not a deterrent but a "proliferant" that goads others to join the club. Arms control has become a way of avoiding a fateful choice: a world of uncontrolled proliferation or a world with no nuclear weapons at all.

*The Folly of Arms Control,* (2000)
Jonathan Schell, American Peace Activist

We got off the train. Tall, strong hard-muscled Americans. Our drill instructors taught us how to march, and how to crawl through machine gun fire. They taught us how to rip out the enemy's throat and how to fire bullets into his brain. Some of these trainees would actually come home like Trumbo's Johnny. Others would die crying for their girlfriends or mothers, mouths clogged with blood and snow, eyes frozen open. All of this would change us. Not for just awhile, but for the rest of our lives. War does that. Gets inside. Doesn't want to leave. I carry it. A discovery, a wound, a challenge. A face that cries for mercy in the world where more than forty armed conflicts are raging.

Philip Berrigan, American Peace Activist (1923-2002)

As a woman, I can't go to war, and I refuse to send anyone else.

Congressional Speech,1941.
Jeannette Rankin, American Politician (1880-1973)

Against all the forces which make for war stands the will to peace. Ever in the background of men's minds is the infinite suffering of war. It kills and maims the best of the race. It brings the deepest of all griefs to every home. It brings poverty and moral degeneration. It brings these poignant ills to victor and vanquished alike.

Herbert Hoover, American President (1874--1964)

The pens which write against disarmament are made with the same steel from which guns are made.
Aristide Briand, French Foreign Minister (1862-1932)

Peace and justice are two sides of the same coin.
Dwight D. Eisenhower, American President (1890-1969)

Nonviolence is the greatest force at the disposal of mankind. It is mightier than the mightiest weapon of destruction devised by the ingenuity of man.
Mahatma Gandhi, Indian Political Leader (1869-1948)

I really see no other solution than to turn inwards and to root out all the rottenness there. I no longer believe that we can change anything in the world until we first change ourselves. And that seems to me the only lesson to be learned from this war.
Etty Hillesum, Dutch Author (1914-1943)

We must be prepared to make heroic sacrifices for the cause of peace that we make ungrudgingly for the cause of war. There is no task that is more important or closer to my heart.
Albert Einstein, German-born American Physicist (1879-1955)

I simply can't build my hopes on a foundation of confusion, misery and death ... I think ... peace and tranquillity will return again.
Anne Frank, German Diarist (1929-1945)

Diplomats are just as essential in starting a war as soldiers are in finishing it. *The Autobiography of Will Rogers.*
Will Rogers, American Humorist (1879-1935)

It is understanding that gives us an ability to have peace. When we understand the other fellow's viewpoint, and he understands ours, then we can sit down and work our differences.

Harry S. Truman, American President (1884-1972)

Universal peace sounds ridiculous to the head of an average family.

Kin Hubbard, American Author (1868-1930)

When I despair, I remember that all through history the way of truth and love has always won. There have been tyrants and murderers and for a time they seem invincible but in the end, they always fall — think of it, ALWAYS!

Mahatma Gandhi,
Indian Political Leader
(1869-1948)

We must face the future more and have wisdom enough to secure peace for our countries and the whole world.

Nikita Khrushchev, Russian Premier (1894-1971)

We will glorify war — the world's only hygiene — militarism, patriotism, the destructive gesture of freedom bringers, beautiful ideas worth dying for, and scorn for women. *Futurist Manifest.*

F.T. Marinetti, Italian Poet (1902-1965)

Right human relations is the only true peace.

Alice A. Bailey, British Author (1880-1949)

For it isn't enough to talk about peace. One must believe in it. And it isn't enough to believe in it. One must work at it.
Eleanor Roosevelt, American Diplomat (1884-1962)

Some things you must always be unable to bear. Some things you must never stop refusing to bear. Injustice and outrage and dishonor and shame. No matter how young you are or how old you have got. Not for kudos and not for cash, your picture in the paper nor money in the bank, neither. Just refuse to bear them.
William Faulkner, American Author (1897-1962)

There is peace in the garden. Peace and results.
Ruth Stout, Dutch Lawyer (1914-1943)

Out of clutter, find simplicity. From discord, find harmony. In the middle of difficulty, lies opportunity.
Albert Einstein, German-born American
Physicist (1879-1955)

Mankind will never win lasting peace so long as men use their full resources only in tasks of war. While we are yet at peace, let us mobilize the potentialities, particularly the moral and spiritual potentialities, which we usually reserve for war.
John Foster Dulles, American Secretary of State
(1888-1959)

Nonviolence is not a garment to be put on and off at will. Its seat is in the heart, and it must be an inseparable part of our being.
Mahatma Gandhi, Indian Political Leader (1869-1948)

Seek peace, and pursue it.
Bible: Proverbs 34:14

It is the job of thinking people, not to be on the side of the executioners.

Albert Camus, French Author (1913-1960)

I know not with what weapons World War III will be fought, but World War IV will be fought with sticks and stones.

Albert Einstein, German-born American
Physicist (1879-1955)

We seek peace, knowing that peace is the climate of freedom. And now, as in no other age, we seek it because we have been warned, by the power of modern weapons, that peace may be the only climate possible for human life itself. "Yet this peace we seek cannot be born of fear alone: it must be rooted in the lives of nations. There must be justice, sensed and shared by all peoples, for without justice the world can know only a tense and unstable truce. There must be law, steadily invoked and respected by all nations, for without law the world promises only such meager justice as the pity of the strong upon the weak. But the law of which we speak, comprehending the values of freedom, affirms the equality of all nations, great and small.

Dwight D. Eisenhower, American President (1890-1969)

I claim to be no more than an average person with less than average ability. I have not the shadow of doubt that any man or woman can achieve what I have, if he or she would make the same effort and cultivate the same hope and faith.

Mahatma Gandhi, Indian Political Leader (1869-1948)

Don't tell me peace has broken out.

Bertold Brecht, German Playwright (1898-1956)

If you oppress poor people, you insult the God who makes them; but kindness shown to the poor is an act of worship.
Bible: Proverbs 14:31

There can never be peace between nations until there is first known that true peace which ... is within the souls of men.
Black Elk, Oglala Sioux Chief (1863-1950)

Nonviolence which is a quality of the heart, cannot come by an appeal to the brain.
Mahatma Gandhi, Indian Political Leader (1869-1948)

Old age should burn and rage at close of day;
Rage, rage against the dying of the light.
*Do not go gentle into that good Night...* (1952)
Dylan Thomas, Welsh Poet (1914-1953)

We will never have true civilization until we have learned to recognize the rights of others.
Will Rogers, American Humorist (1879-1935)

I have great belief in the fact that whenever there is chaos, it creates wonderful thinking. I consider chaos a gift.
Sir Winston Churchill, British Prime Minister(1874-1965)

If we want a free and peaceful world, if we want to make the deserts bloom and man grow to greater dignity as a human being-we can do it.
Eleanor Roosevelt, American Diplomat (1884-1962)

Peace is not only better than war, but infinitely more arduous.
George Bernard Shaw, Irish Author (1856-1950)

You cannot shake hands with a clenched fist.
Indira Gandhi, Indian Prime Minister (1917-1984)

We used to wonder where war lived, what it was that made it so vile. And now we realize that we know where it lives, that it is inside ourselves.
Albert Camus, French Author (1913-1960)

The miracle of the wicked is reinforced by the weakness of the virtuous.
Sir Winston Churchill, British Prime Minister(1874-1965)

I like to believe that people in the long run are going to do more to promote peace than our governments. Indeed, I think that people want peace so much that one of these days governments had better get out of the way and let them have it.
Dwight D. Eisenhower, American President (1890-1969)

You can be killed just as dead in an unjustified war as you can in one protecting your own home.
Will Rogers, American Humorist (1879-1935)

No man can sit down and withhold his hands from the warfare against wrong and get peace from his acquiescence.
Woodrow T. Wilson, American President (1856-1924)

We may never be strong enough to be entirely nonviolent in thought, word and deed. But we must keep nonviolence as our goal and make strong progress towards it. The attainment of freedom, whether for a person, a nation or a world, must be in exact proportion to the attainment of nonviolence for each.
Mahatma Gandhi, Indian Political Leader (1869-1948)

If there is light in the soul, There will be beauty in the person. If there is beauty in the person, There will be harmony in the house. If there is harmony in the house, There will be order in the nation. If there is order in the nation, There will be peace in the world.

Chinese Proverb

Those who can win a war well can rarely make a good peace and those who could make a good peace would never have won the war.
Sir Winston Churchill, British Prime Minister(1874-1965)

We must be the change we wish to see.
Mahatma Gandhi, Indian Political Leader (1869-1948)

Any intelligent fool can make things bigger, more complex, and more violent. It takes a touch of genius — and a lot of courage — to move in the opposite direction.
Albert Einstein, German-born American Physicist
(1879-1955)

You furnish the pictures and I'll furnish the war.
Talking to artist Frederick Remmington in Cuba in 1998
Randolf Hearst, American Newspaper Baron
(1863-1951)

Whenever you are in doubt or when the self becomes too much with you, try the following experiment: Recall the face of the poorest and most helpless person you have ever seen and ask yourself if the step you contemplate is going to be for any use to him or to her Then you will find your doubts and your self melting away.
Mahatma Gandhi, Indian Political Leader (1869-1948)

To get  Peace you must work for Justice.
Paul VI, Italian Pope (1897-1978)

Mankind has grown strong in eternal struggles and it will only perish through eternal peace.

Adolf Hitler, German Chancellor (1889-1945)

He who joyfully marches to music in rank and file has already earned my contempt. He has been given a large brain by mistake, since for him the spinal cord would fully suffice. This disgrace to civilization should be done away with at once. Heroism at command, senseless brutality, deplorable love-of-country stance, how violently I hate all this, how despicable and ignoble war is; I would rather be torn to shreds than be a part of so base an action! It is my conviction that killing under the cloak of war is nothing but an act of murder.

Albert Einstein, German-born American Physicist (1879-1955)

Take diplomacy out of a war and the thing would fall flat in a week.

Will Rogers, American Humorist (1879-1935)

Peace we want because there is another war to fight against poverty, disease and ignorance.

Indira Gandhi, Indian Prime Minister (1917-1984)

Peace is not a relationship of nations. It is a condition of mind brought about by a serenity of soul. Peace is not merely an absence of war. It is also a state of mind. Lasting peace can come only to peaceful people.

Jawaharlal Nehru, Indian Prime Minister (1889-1964)

Until he extends the circle of compassion to all living things, man will not himself find peace.

Dr. Albert Schweitzer, German Missionary (1865-1975)

Every gun that is made, every warship launched, every rocket fired signifies, in the final sense, a theft from those who hunger and are not fed, those who are cold and are not clothed.
Dwight D. Eisenhower, American President (1890-1969)

Each one has to find his peace from within. And peace to be real must be unaffected by outside circumstances.
Mahatma Gandhi, Indian Political Leader (1869-1948)

When peace has been broken anywhere, the peace of all countries is in danger.
Franklin D. Roosevelt, American President (1882-1945)

Peace is not the absence of conflict but the presence of creative alternatives for responding to conflict — alternatives to passive or aggressive responses, alternatives to violence.
Dorothy Thompson, American Journalist (1894-1961)

I object to violence because when it appears to do good, the good is only temporary; the evil it does is permanent.
Mahatma Gandhi, Indian Political Leader (1869-1948)

There's a kind of permission for war which can be given only by the world's mood and atmosphere, the feel of its pulse. It would be madness to undertake a war without that permission. *Tiger at the Gates,* (1935)
Jean Giraudoux, French Diplomat (1882-1944)

Do you want long life and happiness? Strive for peace with all your heart.
Bible: Psalm 34:12,14

If we are to teach real peace in this world, and if we are to carry on a real war against war, we shall have to begin with the children.

Mahatma Gandhi, Indian Political Leader (1869-1948)

In truth, to attain to interior peace, one must be willing to pass through the contrary to peace. Such is the teaching of the Sages.

Swami Brahmanada

Our chiefs are killed ...The little children are freezing to death. My people ... have no blankets, no food ... My heart is sick and sad ... I will fight no more forever.

Joseph, Nez Perce Chief (1840-1904)

The things that will destroy America are prosperity at any price, peace at any price, safety first instead of duty first and love of soft living and the get-rich-quick theory of life.

Theodore Roosevelt, American President (1858-1919)

The true soldier fights not because he hates what is in front of him, but because he loves what is behind him.

Anonymous

We should take care, in inculcating patriotism into our boys and girls, that is a patriotism above the narrow sentiment which usually stops at one's country, and thus inspires jealousy and enmity in dealing with others... Our patriotism should be of the wider, nobler kind which recognises justice and reasonableness in the claims of others and which lead our country into comradeship with...the other nations of the world. The first step to this end is to develop peace and goodwill within our borders, by training our youth of both sexes to its practice as their habit of life, so that the jealousies of town against town, class against class and sect against sect no longer exist; and then to extend this good feeling beyond our frontiers towards our neighbours.

Lord Baden-Powell, British Boy Scout Leader
(1857-1941)

Each religion, by the help of more or less myth which it takes more or less seriously, proposes some method of fortifying the human soul and enabling it to make its peace with its destiny.

George Santayana, Spanish-born American Philosopher
(1863-1952)

Nothing is more important than to war on war.

Leo XIII, Italian Pope (1810-1903)

I am part and parcel of the whole and cannot find God apart from the rest of humanity.

Mahatma Gandhi, Indian Political Leader (1869-1948)

When will our consciences grow so tender that we will act to prevent human misery rather than avenge it?

Eleanor Roosevelt, American Diplomat (1884-1962)

Blessed are the peacemakers, for they shall be called the children of God.

Bible: Matthew 5:3

Every kind of peaceful cooperation among men is primarily based on mutual trust and only secondarily on institutions such as courts of justice and police.

Albert Einstein, German-born American Physicist
(1879-1955)

Be Prepared ... the meaning of the motto is that a scout must prepare himself by previous thinking out and practicing how to act on any accident or emergency so that he is never taken by surprise.

Lord Baden-Powell, British Boy Scout Leader
(1857-1941)

Fear less, hope more,
Whine less, breathe more,
Talk less, say more,
Hate less, love more,
And all good things are yours.

Swedish proverb

I am responsible only to God and history.

Francisco Franco, Spanish General (1892-1975)

There is a price which is too great to pay for peace, and that price can be put in one word. One cannot pay the price of self-respect.

Woodrow T. Wilson, American President (1856-1924)

People talk peace. But men give their life's work to war. It won't stop 'til there is as much brains and scientific study put to aid peace as there is to promote war.

Will Rogers, American Humorist (1879-1935)

Peace is the one condition of survival in this nuclear age.

Adlai Ewing Stevenson, American Vice-President
(1835-1914)

I want to stand by my country, but I cannot vote for war. I vote no.

Congressional speech,1917
Jeannette Rankin, American Politician (1880-1973)

War is the great scavenger of thought. It is the sovereign disinfectant, and its red stream of blood is the Condy's Fluid that cleans out the stagnant pools and clotted channels of the intellect. We have awakened from an opium-dream of comfort, of ease, of that miserable poltroonery of "the sheltered life." Our wish for indulgence of every sort, our laxity of manners, our wretched sensitiveness to personal inconvenience, these are suddenly lifted before us in their true guise as the specters of national decay; and we have risen from the lethargy of our dilettantism to lay them, before it is too late, by the flashing of the unsheathed sword.

Sir Edmund Gosse, British Author (1849-1928)

An eye for eye only ends up making the whole world blind.

Mahatma Gandhi, Indian Political Leader (1869-1948)

When nothing seems to help, I go look at a stonecutter hammering away at a rock perhaps a hundred times without as much as a crack showing in it. Yet at the hundredth blow it will split in two, and I know it was not that blow that did it but all that had gone before.

Jacob Riis, Danish-born American Journalist
(1849-1914)

Technology In health of mind and body, men should see with their own eyes, hear and speak without trumpets, walk on their feet, not on wheels, and work and war with their arms, not with engine-beams, nor rifles warranted to kill twenty men at a shot before you can see them.

John Ruskin, British Author (1819-1900)

The law of violence is not a law, but a simple fact which can only be a law when it does not meet with protest and opposition. It is like the cold, darkness and weight, which people had to put up with until recently when warmth, illumination and leverage were discovered.
Leo Tolstoy, Russian Author (1828-1910)

I don't care how little your country is, you got a right to run it like you want to. When the big nations quit meddling then the world will have peace.'
Will Rogers, American Humorist (1879-1935)

A democracy which makes or even effectively prepares for modern, scientific war must necessarily cease to be democratic. No country can be really well prepared for modern war unless it is governed by a tyrant, at the head of a highly trained and perfectly obedient bureaucracy.
Aldous Huxley, British Author (1894-1963)

The tendency to aggression is an innate, independent, instinctual disposition in man... it constitutes the powerful obstacle to culture.
Sigmund Freud, Austrian Psychiatrist (1856-1939)

But then peace, peace! I am so mistrustful of it: so much afraid that it means a sort of weakness and giving in.
D.H Lawrence, British Author (1885-1930)

If all the Churches of Europe closed their doors until the drums ceased rolling they would act as a most powerful reminder that though the glory of war is a famous and ancient glory, it is not the final glory of God.
George Bernard Shaw, Irish Author (1856-1950)

Don't talk to me about atrocities in war; all war is an atrocity.
> Horatio Kitchener, British General (1850-1916)

The cheapest and most childish of all the taunts of the Pacifists is, I think, the sneer at belligerents for appealing to the God of Battles. It is ludicrously illogical, for we obviously have no right to kill for victory save when we have a right to pray for it. If a war is not a holy war, it is an unholy one — a massacre.
> Gilbert K. Chesterton, British Author (1874-1936)

All violence consists in some people forcing others, under threat of suffering or death, to do what they do not want to do.
> Leo Tolstoy, Russian Author (1828-1910)

The governors of the world believe, and have always believed, that virtue can only be taught by teaching falsehood, and that any man who knew the truth would be wicked. I disbelieve this, absolutely and entirely. I believe that love of truth is the basis of all real virtue, and that virtues based upon lies can only do harm.
> Bertrand Russell, British Philosopher (1872-1970)

It is easier to lead men to combat, stirring up their passion, than to restrain them and direct them toward the patient labors of peace.
> Andre Gide, French Author (1869-1951)

You see things; and you say, "Why?" But I dream things that never were; and I say, "Why not?"
> Also attributed to John F. Kennedy.
> George Bernard Shaw, Irish Author (1856-1950)

Don't ever let them pull you down so low as to hate them. (also cited as: I will permit no man to narrow and degrade my soul by making me hate him.)
Booker T. Washington, American Educator (1856-1915)

War makes good history but peace is poor reading.
Thomas Hardy, British Author (1840-1928)

Bless your persecutors; bless and do not curse them. Rejoice with those who rejoice, weep with those who weep. Have the same attitude toward all. Put away ambitious thoughts and associate with those who are lowly. Would that even today you knew the things that make for peace.
Bible: Luke 19:42

If I can stop one heart from breaking, I shall not live in vain.
Emily Dickinson, American Poet (1830-1886)

Wars are not acts of God. They are caused by man, by man-made institutions, by the way in which man has organized his society. What man has made, man can change.
Frederick Moore Vinson, American Chief Justice (1890-1953)

Why does man have reason if he can only be influenced by violence?
Leo Tolstoy, Russian Author (1828-1910)

Men are so accustomed to maintaining external order by violence that they cannot conceive of life being possible without violence.
Leo Tolstoy, Russian Author (1828-1910)

The philosophers have only interpreted the world, in various ways: the point is to change it.
Karl Marx, German Philosopher (1818-1883)

How good bad music and bad reasons sound when we march against an enemy.
Fredirich Nietzsche, German Philosopher (1844-1900)

Non-violence leads to the highest ethics, which is the goal of all evolution. Until we stop harming all other living beings, we are still savages.
Thomas Edison, American Scientist (1847-1931)

We love peace, but not peace at any price. There is a peace more destructive of the manhood of living man, than war is destructive to his body. Chains are worse than bayonets.
Douglas Jerrold, British Journalist (1803-1857)

The United States is not a nation to which peace is a necessity.
Grover Cleveland, American President (1837-1908)

In truth, to attain to interior peace, one must be willing to pass through the contrary to peace. Such is the teaching of the Sages.
Swami Brahmanada, Indian Mystic (1863-1922)

War does not determine who is right — only who is left
Bertrand Russell, British Philosopher (1872-1970)

All men love peace in their armchairs after dinner; but they disbelieve the other nations's professions, rightly measuring its sincerity by their own.
Oscar W. Firkins

One must care about a world one will never see.
Bertrand Russell, British Philosopher (1872-1970)

When it's a question of peace one must talk to the Devil himself.
Edouard Herriot, French Prime Minister (1872-1957)

Murder and capital punishment are not opposites that cancel one another, but similars that breed their kind. It is the deed that teaches not the name we give it.
George Bernard Shaw, Irish Author (1856-1950)

Thaw with her gentle persuasion is more powerful than Thor with his hammer. The one melts, the other breaks into pieces.
Henry David Thoreau, American Author (1817-1862)

Am I not destroying my enemies while I make friends of them?
Abraham Lincoln, American President (1809-1865)

Whatever you do, you need courage. Whatever course you decide upon, there is always someone to tell you that you are wrong. There are always difficulties arising that tempt you to believe your critics are right. To map out a course of action and follow it to an end requires some of the same courage that a soldier needs. Peace has its victories, but it takes brave men and women to win them.
Ralph Waldo Emerson, American Poet (1802-1882)

If we could read the secret history of our enemies, we should find in each life sorrow and suffering enough to disarm all hostility.

Henry Wadsworth Longfellow, American Poet (1807-1882)

Violence produces only something resembling justice, but it distances people from the possibility of living justly, without violence.

Leo Tolstoy, Russian Author (1828-1910)

Peace is the first thing the angels sang.

John Keble, British Clergyman (1792-1866)

I hope ... that mankind will at length, as they call themselves reasonable creatures, have reason and sense enough to settle their differences without cutting throats; for in my opinion there never was a good war, or a bad peace.

Benjamin Franklin, American Statesman (1706-1790)

Peace, plenty, and contentment reign throughout our borders, and our beloved country presents a sublime moral spectacle to the world.

James Knox Polk, American President (1795-1849)

Why should we be in such desperate haste to succeed and in such desperate enterprises? If a man does not keep pace with his companions, perhaps it is because he hears a different drummer. Let him step to the music which he hears, however measured or far away.

Henry David Thoreau, American Author (1817-1862)

Nothing can bring you peace but yourself.

Ralph Waldo Emerson, American Poet (1802-1882)

We feel that our cause is just and holy; we protest solemnly in the face of mankind that we desire peace at any sacrifice save that of honour and independence; we ask no conquest, no aggrandizement, no concession of any kind from the States with which we were lately confederated; all we ask is to be let alone; that those who never held power over us shall not now attempt our subjugation by arms.
Jefferson Davis, American Statesman (1808-1889)

Change is certain. Peace is followed by disturbances; departure of evil men by their return. Such recurrences should not constitute occasions for sadness but realities for awareness, so that one may be happy in the interim.
Percy Bysshe Shelley, British Poet (1792-1822)

If they want peace, nations should avoid the pin-pricks that precede cannon shots.
Napoleon Bonaparte, French Emperor (1769-1821)

When we treat man as he is, we make him worse than he is; when we treat him as if he already were what he potentially could be, we make him what he should be.
Johann Wolfgang von Goethe, German Poet (1749-1842)

What good is a house, if you haven't got a decent planet to put it on?
Henry David Thoreau, American Author (1817-1862)

I expect to pass through this world but once, therefore any good that I can do, or any kindness that I can show to any fellow creature, let me do it now; let me not defer it or neglect it, for I shall not come this way again.
Stephen Grellett, French Quaker Minister (1773-1855)

Peace hath higher tests of manhood than battle ever knew.
John Greenleaf Whittier, American Poet (1807-1892)

Peace is rarely denied to the peaceful.
Friedrich von Schiller, German Poet (1759-1805)

The first thing to be disrupted by our commitment to nonviolence will be not the system but our own lives.
James Douglass, American Poet (1762-1851)

Can I see another's woe, and not be in sorrow too?
Can I see another's grief, and not seek for kind relief?
William Blake, British Poet (1757-1827)

Peace and friendship with all mankind is our wisest policy, and I wish we may be permitted to pursue it.
Thomas Jefferson, American President (1743-1826)

Peace cannot be achieved through violence, it can only be attained through understanding
Ralph Waldo Emerson, American Poet (1802-1882)

Of all the evils to public liberty, war is perhaps the most to be dreaded.
James Madison, American President (1751-1836)

To see the world in a grain of sand and heaven in a wild flower, hold infinity in the palm of your hand and eternity in an hour.
William Blake, British Poet (1757-1827)

On all the peaks lies peace.
Johann Wolfgang von Goethe, German Poet (1749-1842)

It is reasonable that every one who asks justice should do justice.
Thomas Jefferson, American President (1743-1826)

For every minute you remain angry, you give up sixty seconds of peace of mind.
Ralph Waldo Emerson, American Poet (1802-1882)

.

Nothing is more conducive to peace of mind than not having any opinions at all.
Georg Christopher Lichtenberg, German Physicist (1742-1799)

If there must be trouble, let it be in my day, that my child may have peace.
Thomas Paine, British Author (1737-1809)

Wars begin in the minds of men, and in those minds, love and compassion would have built the defenses of peace.
Thomas Jefferson, American President (1743-1826)

Nothing can bring you peace but yourself.
Ralph Waldo Emerson, American Poet (1802-1882)

I must study war and politics so that my children shall be free to study commerce, agriculture and other practicalities, so that their children can study painting, poetry and other fine things.
John Adams, American President (1735-1826)

Observe good faith and justice toward all nations. Cultivate peace and harmony with all.
George Washington, American President (1732-1799)

Virtue is more to be feared than vice, because its excesses are not subject to the regulation of conscience.
Adam Smith, British Philospher (1723-1790)

My first wish is to see this plague to mankind [war] banished from off this earth.
George Washington, American President (1732-1799)

He that would live in peace and at ease must not speak all he knows or all he sees.
Benjamin Franklin, American Politician (1706-1790)

Even peace may be purchased at too high a price.
Benjamin Franklin, American Statesman (1706-1790)

When I have money, I get rid of it quickly, lest it find a way into my heart.
John Wesley, British Methodist Minister (1703-1791)

Those who can make you believe absurdities can make you commit atrocities.
Voltaire, (Francois Marie Arouet) French Philosopher (1694-1778)

Peace does not dwell in outward things, but within the soul; we may preserve it in the midst of the bitterest pain, if our will remains firm and submissive. Peace in this life springs from acquiescence not in an exemption from suffering.
François Fenelon, French Bishop (1651-1715)

Peace is not an absence of war, it is a virtue, a state of mind, a disposition for benevolence, confidence, justice.
Baruch Spinoza, Dutch Philosopher (1632-1677)

If I have been able to see further, it was only because I stood on the shoulders of giants.
Sir Isaac Newton, British Scientist (1642-1727)

To be at peace in crime! ah, who can thus flatter himself.
Voltaire, (Francois Marie Arouet) French Philosopher (1694-1778)

We utterly deny all outward wars and strife, and fightings with outward weapons, for any end, or under any pretense whatsoever; this is our testimony to the whole world ... The Spirit of Christ, by which we are guided, is not changeable, so as once to command us from a thing as evil, and again to move unto it; and we certainly know, and testify to the world, that the Spirit of Christ, which leads us into all truth, will never move us to fight and war against any man with outward weapons, neither for the Kingdom of Christ nor for the kingdoms of this world ... Therefore, we cannot learn war any more.
*Declaration of Morman Friends* to King Charles II (1630-1685)

If you would be a real seeker after truth, it is necessary that at least once in your life you doubt, as far as possible, all things.
René Descartes, French Philosopher (1596-1650)

Chase brave employment with a naked sword. Throughout the world. *The Church Porch.*
George Herbert, Welsh Poet (1593-1633)

Never be in a hurry; do everything quietly and in a calm spirit. Do not lose your inner peace for anything whatsoever, even if your whole world seems upset.
St. Francis de Sales, Bishop of Geneva (1567-1622)

I am a peace-loving man. I believe that it ought to be the first wish of every honest man to live in tranquility of mind ... I am sorry that all kings and princes are not of this humor.

> Peter Paul Rubens, Dutch Painter (1577-1640)

Peace is produced by war.

> Pierre Corneille, French Dramatist (1606-1684)

A peace is of the nature of a conquest; for then both parties nobly are subdued, and neither party loser.

> William Shakespeare, British Playwright (1564-1616)

Force, and fraud, are in war the two cardinal virtues.

> Thomas Hobbes, British Philosopher (1588-1679)

I do not feel obliged to believe that the same god who has endowed us with sense, reason and intellect has intended us to forgo their use.

> Galileo Galilei, Italian Astronomer (1564-1642)

No man is an island entire of itself ... any man's death diminishes me because I am involved in mankind; and therefore never send to know for whom the bell tolls; **it** tolls for thee.

> John Donne, British Poet (1572-1631)

In the twilight of life, God will not judge us on our earthly possessions and human success, but rather on how much we have loved.

> St. John of the Cross, Italian Saint (1542-1591)

No enterprise is more likely to succeed than one concealed from the enemy until it is ripe for execution.

> Niccolo Machiavelli, Italian Statesman (1469-1527)

170

Since we are to be conformed to the image of Christ, how can we then fight our enemies with the sword? ... Spears and swords of iron we leave to those who, alas, consider human blood and swine's blood of well-nigh equal value.

Menno Simons, Dutch Priest (1496-1561)

War makes thieves and peace hangs them.

George Herbert, Welsh Poet (1593-1633)

Peace is more important than all justice; and peace was not made for the sake of justice, but justice for the sake of peace.

Martin Luther, German Religious Leader (1483-1546)

Nothing good ever comes of violence.

Martin Luther, German Religious Leader (1483-1546)

Truly man is the king of beasts, for his brutality exceeds them. We live by the death of others. We are burial places! I have from an early age abjured the use of meat, and the time will come when men such as I will look upon the murder of animals as they now look on the murder of men.

Leonardo da Vinci, Italian Painter (1452-1519)

The most disadvantageous peace is better than the most just war.

Desiderius Erasmus, Dutch Scholar (1466-1536)

When the soul is naughted and transformed, then of herself she neither works nor speaks nor wills, nor feels nor hears nor understands; neither has she of herself the feeling of outward or inward, where she may move. And in all things it is God who rules and guides her,

171

without the meditation of any creature ... And she is so full of peace that thought she pressed her flesh, her nerves, her bones, no other thing come forth from them than peace.

St. Catherine of Genoa, Italian Saint (1447-1510)

First keep the peace within yourself, then you can also bring peace to others.

Thomas á Kempis, German Monk (1380-1471)

Do not be wise in your own estimation. Never repay injury with injury. See that your conduct is honorable in the eyes of all. If possible, live peacefully with everyone. Beloved, do not avenge yourselves; leave that to God's wrath, for it is written, "Vengeance is mine; I will repay."

Francesco Petrarch, Italian Poet (1304-1374)

Five enemies of peace inhabit with us — avarice, ambition, envy, anger, and pride; if these were to be banished, we should infallibly enjoy perpetual peace.

Francesco Petrarch, Italian Poet, (1304-1374)

A peace that comes from fear and not from the heart is the opposite of peace.

Levi ben Gershon, French Philosopher
(1288-1344)

Peace is the work of justice indirectly, in so far as justice removes the obstacles to peace; but it is the work of charity (love) directly, since charity, according to its own notion, causes peace.

Thomas Aquinas, Italian Philosopher (1225-1274)

While you are proclaiming peace with your lips, be careful to have it even more fully in your heart.

Francis of Assisi, Italian Saint (1181-1226)

Grant that I may not so much seek to be understood as to understand.

Francis of Assisi, Italian Saint (1181-1226)

Not to hurt our humble brethren (the animals) is our first duty to them, but to stop there is not enough. We have a higher mission — to be of service to them whenever they require it ... If you have men who will exclude any of God's creatures from the shelter of compassion and pity, you will have men who will deal likewise with their fellow men.

Francis of Assisi, Italian Saint (1181-1226)

God grant me the courage to change the things I can, the patience to accept the things I can't, and the wisdom to know the difference. *The Serenity Prayer.*

Connsidered to have been written by a philosopher Boethius (480-524 AD)

Of war men ask the outcome, not the cause.

Lucius Annaeus Seneca, Greek Statesman (c.4 BC-65 AD)

Peace can be reached through meditation on the knowledge which dreams give. Peace can also be reached through concentration upon that which is dearest to the heart.

Patanjali, Indian Yogi Founder (c. 500 BC)

If you live alone, whose feet will you wash?

Basil the Great, Turkish Priest (c.329-379 AD)

In the absence of justice, what is sovereignty but organized robbery?

St. Augustine, Italian Saint (c.354-430 AD)

When someone steals another's clothes, we call them a thief. Should we not give the same name to one who could clothe the naked and does not? The bread in your cupboard belongs to the hungry; the coat unused in your closet belongs to the one who needs it; the shoes rotting in your closet belong to the one who has no shoes; the money which you hoard up belongs to the poor.
Basil the Great,Turkish Priest (c.329-379 AD)

Taking the first footstep with a good thought, the second with a good word, and the third with a good deed, I entered paradise.
Zoroaster. Persian Prophet (c.630-550 BC)

No one would be foolish enough to choose war over peace — in peace sons bury their fathers, but in war fathers bury their sons.
Croesus of Lydia, King of Persia (c.560-546 BC)

Peace comes from within. Do not seek it without.
Buddha (Siddhartha Gautama) (c.563-483 BC)

In separateness lies the world's great misery; in compassion lies the world's true strength.
Buddha (Siddhartha Gautama) (c.563-483 BC)

Better than a thousand hollow words, Is one word that brings peace.
Buddha (Siddhartha Gautama) (c.563-483 BC)

Teach this triple truth to all: A generous heart, kind speech, and a life of service and compassion are the things which renew humanity.
Buddha (Siddhartha Gautama) (c.563-483 BC)

Everything is changeable, everything appears and disappears; there is no blissful peace until one passes beyond the agony of life and death.

Buddha
(Siddhartha Gautama)
(c.563-483 BC)

For as long as men massacre animals, they will kill each other. Indeed, he who sows the seed of murder and pain cannot reap joy and love.

Pythagoras, Greek Philosopher (c.582-500 BC)

It is only necessary to make war with five things; with the maladies of the body, the ignorantness of the mind, with the passions of the body, with the sedition of the city, and the discords of families.

Pythagoras, Greek Philosopher (c.582-500 BC)

What you do not want done to yourself, do not do unto others.

Confucius, Chinese Philsopher (c.551-479 BC)

To know what is right and not to do it is the worst cowardice.

Confucius, Chinese Philsopher (c.551-479 BC)

To fight and conquer in all our battles is not supreme excellence; supreme excellence consists in breaking the enemy's resistance without fighting.

Sun Tzu Wu, Chinese War Lord (c.514-496 BC)

A crust eaten in peace is better than a banquet partaken in anxiety.

> Aesop, Greek Philosopher (c.620-560 BC)

He who does not attempt to make peace when small discords arise, Is like the bee's hive which leaks drops of honey Soon, the whole hive collapses.

> Siddha Nagarjuna (c.100-200 AD)

Lord, make me an instrument of your peace.
Where there is hatred, let me sow love,
Where there is injury, pardon,
Where there is doubt, faith,
Where there is despair, hope,
Where there is darkness, light,
where there is sadness, joy.

O Divine Master,
grant that I may not so much seek
To be consoled as to console,
To be understood as to understand,
To be loved as to love.
For it is in giving that we receive,
It is in pardoning that we are pardoned,
It is in dying that we are born to eternal life.

> The Prayer of St. Francis

Let us know peace.
For as long as the moon shall rise,
For as long as the rivers shall flow,
For as long as the sun will shine,
For as long as the grass shall grow,
Let us know peace.

> A Native American Prayer by a Cheyenne Indian

# INDEX

182

186

*Catch 22,* by Joseph Heller, © Simon & Schuster, 1961
*All Too Human,* by George Stephanopoulos, © Little Brown
& Co. New York 1999
Kafka novel. *The Match,* No 79, by Fred Woodworth.
*Anarchy in Action,* by Colin Ward, © George Allen &
Unwin 1973
*Hiroshima, The Nuclear Predicament,* © Jonathan Schell,
1986
*The Folly of Arms Control,* (2000) © Jonathan Schell
*The Dancing Mind,* by Toni Morrison, © Alfred Knopf,
1996
*To Have or to Be?* by Erich Fromm,© Bantam
*The New Penguin Dictionary of Modern
Quotations,* by Robert Andrews © Penguin, 2000
*Dictionary of Quotations,* 2nd Edition,
© Oxford University Press, 1953
*Bartlett's Familiar Quotations,* by John Bartlett & Justin
Kaplan, © Little Brown & Co. Boston 1992

The following Publishers:
Rupert Hart-Davis
The Citadel Press
Grove Press
Harper Collins
Jonathan Cape
The Viking Press
Harper Colophon
Holt Rinehart & Winston

*Newsweek*
*Montreal Gazette*

www.nhpeaceaction.org
www.freespace.virgin.net
www.womenshistory.about.com
www.1-famous-quotes.com
www.Historical_quotes.htm
www.brainyquotes.com
www.bartleby.com
www.quotelady.com
www.satirewire.com
www.great-quotes.com
www.ppu.org.uk
www.wagingpeace.org
www.internationalanswer.org

The Publisher welcomes any information regarding errors or omissions, that we may make necessary corrections in subsequent printings.

First published in Canada by
**Sound And Vision**
359 Riverdale Avenue
Toronto, Canada, M4J 1A4
www.soundandvision.com

First printing, July 2003
1 3 5 7 9 - printings - 10 8 6 4 2


**National Library of Canada Cataloguing in
Publication Data**

Quotable war or peace / [compiled by] Geoff Savage
Includes index.
ISBN 0-920151-57-4
1. War—Quotations, maxims, etc.  2. Peace—
Quotations, maxims, etc.  I. Savage, Geoff, 1945-

PN6084.W35Q67 2003  808.88'2  C2003-903557-3

Typeset in ITC Souvenir
Printed and bound in Canada by Metrolitho Inc,.

*Quotable Pop*
Fifty Decades of Blah Blah Blah
Compiled & Edited by Phil Dellio & Scott Woods
Caricatures by Mike Rooth
isbn 0-920151-50-7

*Quotable Jazz*
Compiled & Edited by Marshall Bowden
Caricatures by Mike Rooth
isbn 0-920151-55-8

*Quotable Opera*
Compiled & Edited by Steve & Nancy Tanner
Caricatures by Umberto Tàccola
isbn 0-920151-54-X

*Quotable Alice*
Compiled & Edited by David W. Barber
Illustrations by Sir John Tenniel
isbn 0-920151-52-3

*Quotable Sherlock*
Compiled & Edited by David W. Barber
Illustrations by Sidney Paget
isbn 0-920151-53-1

*Quotable Twain*
Compiled & Edited by David W. Barber
isbn 0-920151-56-6

Titles by David W. Barber,
with cartoons by Dave Donald:

*A Musician's Dictionary*
preface by Yehudi Menuhin
isbn 0-920151-21-3

*Bach, Beethoven and the Boys*
Music History as It Ought to Be Taught
preface by Anthony Burgess
isbn 0-920151-10-8

*When the Fat Lady Sings*
Opera History as It Ought to Be Taught
preface by Maureen Forrester
foreword by Anna Russell
isbn 0-920151-34-5

*If It Ain't Baroque*
More Music History as It Ought to Be Taught
isbn 0-920151-15-9

*Tenors, Tantrums and Trills*
An Opera Dictionary from Aida to Zzzz
isbn 0-920151-19-1

*Tutus, Tights and Tiptoes*
Ballet History as It Ought to Be Taught
preface by Karen Kain
isbn 0-920151-30-2

Compiled & Edited by
David W. Barber
*Better Than It Sounds*
A Dictionary of Humorous Musical Quotations
isbn 0-920151-22-1

Compiled & Edited by
David W. Barber
*The Music Lover's Quotation Book*
isbn 0-920151-37-X

*The Composers*
A Hystery of Music
by Kevin Reeves
preface by Daniel Taylor
isbn 0-920151-29-9

*1812 And All That*
A Concise History of Music from 30.000 BC
to the Millennium
by Lawrence Leonard,
cartoons by Emma Bebbington
isbn 0-920151-33-7

*How to Stay Awake*
During Anybody's Second Movement
by David E. Walden, cartoons by Mike Duncan
preface by Charlie Farquharson
isbn 0-920151-20-5

*How To Listen To Modern Music*
Without Earplugs
by David E. Walden, cartoons by Mike Duncan
foreword by Bramwell Tovey
isbn 0-920151-31-0

*The Thing I've Played With the Most*
Professor Anthon E. Darling Discusses
His Favourite Instrument
by David E. Walden, cartoons by Mike Duncan
foreword by Mabel May Squinnge, B.O.
isbn 0-920151-35-3

*Love Lives of the Great Composers*
From Gesualdo to Wagner
by Basil Howitt
isbn 0-920151-18-3

*More Love Lives of the Great Composers*
by Basil Howitt
isbn 0-920151-36-1

*Opera Antics & Annecdotes*
by Stephen Tanner
Illustrations by Umberto Táccola
preface by David W. Barber
isbn 0-920151-32-9

*I Wanna Be Sedated*
Pop Music in the Seventies
by Phil Dellio & Scott Woods
Caricatures by Dave Prothero
preface by Chuck Eddy
isbn 0-920151-16-7

*A Working Musician's Joke Book*
by Daniel G. Theaker
Cartoons by Mike Freen
preface by David Barber
isbn o-920151-23-X

## A Note from the Publisher

I would like thank the following people:

Bruce Surtees for writing the preface for my book. I have known Bruce since I started in this crazy business way back in 1967. He was the proprietor of the Book Cellar, the best book store in Toronto at the time. A special thanks to Mike 'Eagle Eye' Walsh for his invaluable editorial advice and friendship over the years. Thanks again to David Barber for his continuing original work. It's a joy to collaborate with such professional people.

When I started Sound And Vision in 1983, I was able to find two great distributors: Lionel Koffler at Firefly Books and John Loweth at Mayfair Music.

My mandate has always been to publish books for the international market and also to sell foreign rights. I have been successful over the years in finding European publishers who have successfully translated a number of our titles. This year I'm pleased to see our books are being translated and published in China.

Lastly I would like to thank all the customers for purchasing our books.

Geoff Savage